BETWEEN FRIENDS

◆

PERSPECTIVES ON
JOHN KENNETH GALBRAITH

Between Friends

PERSPECTIVES ON

John Kenneth Galbraith

With essays by:
DEREK BOK · CARLOS FUENTES
PETER GALBRAITH · KATHARINE GRAHAM
ROBERT HEILBRONER · WILL HUTTON
ROY JENKINS · STEPHEN A. MARGLIN
DANIEL PATRICK MOYNIHAN · RICHARD PARKER
ROBERT B. REICH · MICHEL ROCARD
ERIC ROLL · AMARTYA SEN
ARTHUR M. SCHLESINGER, JR.
STUART CARY WELCH
ANDREA WILLIAMS

Editor: HELEN SASSON
Associate Editor: ANDREA WILLIAMS

Houghton Mifflin Company   BOSTON   NEW YORK   1999

Library of Congress Cataloging-in-Publication Data is available.
ISBN 0-395-97130-6

Book design by Anne Chalmers
Typeface: New Baskerville (Adobe) and Monotype Baskerville

PRINTED IN THE UNITED STATES OF AMERICA
HAD 10 9 8 7 6 5 4 3 2 1

CONTENTS

◆

*On Galbraith's economic, social,
and political ideas*

INTRODUCTION

◆

I<small>T IS WITH CONSIDERABLE PLEASURE</small> that I introduce
this collection of essays written to honor the ninetieth birthday of John Kenneth Galbraith, one of the world's most
famous economists.

John Kenneth Galbraith's economic ideas have been extensively analyzed in many books and publications, and
were also the subject of a collection of essays by eminent
economists to honor an earlier birthday: *Unconventional Wisdom*, published by Houghton Mifflin.

My idea for this celebratory volume, therefore, was to invite Kenneth Galbraith's friends to write about him in a
much broader context and in many of his aspects. The wide
array of distinguished contributors who honor him in these
pages thus reflects the richness and the breadth of his life
and his ideas—not only as an economist, but also as a
teacher, a writer, a public servant and ambassador, a collector
of Indian art, and the head of a gifted family.

The contributors have written about Kenneth Galbraith
from their own highly individual perspectives in politics,
journalism, economics and academia, the world of art, or
just as his good friends. Their style is anecdotal, biographi-
cal, and analytical and often a mixture of all three, and their
contributions have broadly fallen into two groups. In the
first, the essays are about Galbraith as a person, about some

of the major events in his life, and how the authors believe these have influenced the development of his ideas. The second group of essays is about Galbraith's economic and political ideas and his major books; the authors here examine how these have stood the test of time and how they themselves have been influenced by them. It was the wish of the contributors, and myself, that Galbraith should also join us in these pages, and Andrea Williams has made this possible with "Galbraith on Galbraith," the concluding chapter to this collection.

It seemed appropriate to begin with the poetic essay "A Quixote of the Plains" by Carlos Fuentes, in which he so beautifully epitomizes Galbraith's ideas and characteristics. The essays by Peter Galbraith, his son, and by Daniel Patrick Moynihan, his former neighbor, follow. The sequence in the first section, then, is by authors who have known him longest, thus starting with the earlier phases of Galbraith's life.

Carlos Fuentes's essay is about Galbraith's humanity. He writes of him as an economist who has placed the pursuit of social justice, so often neglected by his profession, at the basis of his economic ideas.

Peter Galbraith describes the lessons he learned from his father's experiences as Ambassador to India and how these served him so well during his own posting as Ambassador to Croatia. He compares some of the key political events in India that Kenneth Galbraith faced with how he himself coped with the tumultuous times in Croatia.

Daniel Patrick Moynihan succeeded Galbraith as Ambassador to India some ten years later. His essay is a personal and entertaining account of Galbraith as his neighbor of many years in Cambridge, Massachusetts.

Eric Roll writes of his friendship with Galbraith since 1939 and discusses some of the events in the earlier period of their friendship which were to influence Galbraith in later years. He believes that two were of particular significance to his development: Galbraith's involvement in the administration of the war effort gave him the insights into bureaucracies and large corporations which helped form some of the ideas he later developed in *The Affluent Society* and *The New Industrial State*. Galbraith's next experience as the editor of *Fortune* magazine refined his writing skills.

How this experience liberated Galbraith's literary style to become the exuberant and witty writing of his many later books is also mentioned by Arthur Schlesinger in the next essay. Schlesinger, whose friendship with Galbraith began in 1943, moves us on to the important role that politics has played in Galbraith's life, and with a political historian's eye, he explains how central this is to Galbraith's economic and social ideas. Schlesinger is also able to tell us, from the vantage he later had as a prominent member of the Kennedy Administration, about Galbraith's friendship with Kennedy, which saw Galbraith at the height of his political influence and also gave him much material for his later writing.

In his anecdotal essay, Roy Jenkins generously introduces us to the Galbraith he has grown to know through their forty-five years of friendship. Galbraith's famous wit, self-confidence, and generosity are portrayed, as are their exchanges on American and British party politics and, more amusingly, on politicians.

There are further glimpses, by his longtime friend Katharine Graham, of Galbraith's political life in Washington, where he and Schlesinger were Adlai Stevenson's and, later, Kennedy's speechwriters. She writes of his outspokenness, which provoked the more conservative economists in the Kennedy Administration, fearful of his influence, to devise a "system" to alert them to his visits from New Delhi. She also writes of their correspondence, in which he advised and lectured her on her role and responsibilities as a newspaper publisher.

Galbraith has spent fifty years of his life at Harvard University, intermittently interrupted by his political and other activities, and Derek Bok, who was President of Harvard University for twenty of those years, tells us of the intellectual distinction that Galbraith has brought to the university, his often controversial stance, his loyalty, his role in the continuing enhancement of Harvard's quality and values, and his great generosity to the university. This included the gift of his superb collection of Indian miniature paintings.

The curator of Harvard's Fogg Museum, Cary Welch, who was closely involved with that bequest, recounts how Galbraith's aesthetic taste developed in India and how it is reflected in the pictures he collected.

Will Hutton discusses why he believes that the pendulum has begun to swing back to Galbraith's values and economic philosophy. The events in Asia, with their great dangers for the destabilization of the Western economies and the world financial system, reminiscent of Galbraith's famous book, *The Great Crash 1929*, are demonstrating that unregulated markets internationally—and domestically, in some of the Asian economies—are unlikely to be able to redress the deepening crisis, and that greater control, frequently advocated by Galbraith, may be needed. There is also a move away from unbridled capitalism in the United States and Britain, with a search for "third way" social policies, and Hutton discusses whether these are likely to measure up to Galbraith's social and political ideas.

Robert Reich, in his essay, is pessimistic about the ability of current domestic social policies to deal with the inequalities of modern society, and questions how today, forty years after the publication of Galbraith's *The Affluent Society,* in which a world of material plenty was anticipated, a significant number of Americans are poorer than ever. He believes that Galbraith himself, in his later books, has grown less optimistic as to the future social outcome.

Robert Heilbroner considers that the accessibility of Galbraith's writings to a wide public has greatly contributed to an awareness of the material inequalities that exist in America. Heilbroner contends that Galbraith, as Keynes had done before him, changed public attitudes toward economics, but that whereas Keynes's target was political, Galbraith's is moral.

Michel Rocard writes on the importance to him of Galbraith's ideas and books and how they have helped him, a French social democrat, to articulate the past mistakes made by his own party. He also speaks of Galbraith's ideas on mass poverty and how they have contributed to his own personal views on the policies that are needed to help its eradication.

Galbraith's contributions to economics are examined in a scholarly essay by Stephen Marglin. It focuses on the ideas Galbraith presented in his two landmark books, *The Affluent Society* and *The New Industrial State.* Marglin analyzes Galbraith's achievements and examines the validity in today's circumstances of the ideas expressed in these works. He argues that a truer test of the Galbraithian achievement would be to examine the manner in which Galbraith faced the *foundational* assumptions and *economic myths* (individualism, unlimited wants, self-interest, rationality) underlying mainstream economics and how Galbraith challenged their validity as a descriptive framework in which to fashion a true reflection of the economic world, and he proceeds to do this.

Amartya Sen writes about Galbraith's work from the viewpoint of the methodology of economics and about Galbraith's analytical and diagnostic skills, which have resulted in his far-reaching insights into society. He also discusses these in relation to Galbraith's analysis of Indian society and art.

Richard Parker's essay is about some of the early influences on Galbraith's economic and political ideas. Galbraith himself has acknowledged, as have many commentators and critics, the strong influence that Maynard Keynes and Thorstein Veblen had on his ideas. Parker, however, argues that Galbraith was also greatly influenced by the earlier ideas of the highly pragmatic "German" tradition in economics, brought back to America at the end of the nineteenth century. He also describes how important were the influences of the political ideas and activities of Galbraith's father on his son.

In the concluding chapter to this volume, Andrea Williams has selected aphorisms and brief passages from some of Galbraith's best-known books in which she believes that he "reveals more about himself than he may know."

These essays are being published in the hope that Kenneth Galbraith's pleasure in reading them will equal that of their authors in writing their tributes to him. The warm affection and regard they express for him is in no less measure shared by the editor, who treasures and looks forward to many more years of his friendship.

—HELEN SASSON,
London, August 1998

THE CONTRIBUTORS

———◆———

DEREK BOK was President of Harvard University and, before that, Dean of the Harvard Law School. He currently serves as 300th Anniversary University Professor at Harvard and continues to teach at the Kennedy School of Government. His current research interests include the state of higher education, also the subject of his most recent book, *The State of the Nation.*

CARLOS FUENTES is one of Mexico's most renowned authors. He is a former Ambassador to France and has taught at many universities, including Harvard and Cambridge. He is the author of numerous novels, short stories, and essays, and is the recipient of the Cervantes de Asturias Prizes (Spain) and the National Award for Literature (Mexico).

PETER GALBRAITH was, until January 1998, American Ambassador to Croatia. Prior to that he spent fourteen years with the Senate Foreign Relations Committee, soon after graduating from Harvard and Oxford universities.

KATHARINE GRAHAM is Chairman of the Executive Committee of the Washington Post Company. She is also vice chairman of the board of the Urban Institute and a member of the Council on Foreign Relations and the Overseas

Development Council. She is a fellow of the American Academy of Arts and Sciences and author of *Personal History*, her memoirs, published in 1997.

ROBERT HEILBRONER has written some twenty books, including *The Worldly Philosophers*, published when he was a graduate student at the New School for Social Research, where he is now Professor Emeritus.

WILL HUTTON is one of Britain's leading economic journalists. He is editor-in-chief of *The Observer* and was also, for a number of years, a producer and correspondent with the BBC. His book *The State We're In* has been on the best-seller list ever since it was published in 1995. *The State to Come* was published in 1997. He is on the board of the London School of Economics.

ROY JENKINS (Lord Jenkins of Hillhead) is Chancellor of the University of Oxford and is currently heading the commission on British electoral reform. He is a former Chancellor of the Exchequer, co-founder of the Social Democratic Party, and former President of the European Commission. He has written many political biographies, including, in 1997, *Gladstone*.

DANIEL PATRICK MOYNIHAN is U.S. Senator from the State of New York. He is a former American Ambassador to India and Permanent Representative of the United States to the United Nations. He served in the Cabinet and sub-Cabinets of Presidents Kennedy, Johnson, Nixon, and Ford, and has also been a professor at Harvard University. His most recent book is *Secrecy: The American Experience* (1998).

RICHARD PARKER is an Oxford-trained economist and former journalist. He now teaches at Harvard's Kennedy School of Government, where he is a Senior Fellow in the Shorenstein Center on the Press, Politics, and Public Policy, and Director of the Program on Economics and Journalism.

STEPHEN A. MARGLIN holds the Walter S. Barker Chair in the Department of Economics at Harvard University. His current research focuses on the foundational assumptions of economics, and to what extent these assumptions are a reflection of the culture and history of the modern West rather than a set of facts about a universal human nature, and what difference it makes.

ROBERT B. REICH is University Professor and the Maurice Hexter Professor of Social and Economic Policy at Brandeis University. He served as Secretary of Labor in the first Clinton Administration

MICHEL ROCARD was Prime Minister of France from 1988 to 1991 and Secretary of the French Socialist Party until 1994. He is a member of the European Parliament, in which he heads the Commission of Development. He is also a former Mayor and resigned as a Senator in the French Assembly in 1997. He is the author of numerous publications in French.

ERIC ROLL (Lord Roll of Ipsden) was President of S. G. Warburg & Co., the merchant bank, until 1995 and is Senior Adviser to Warburg Dillon Read. He is a former British Permanent Undersecretary of State and professor of economics. He is the author of numerous books, including *A History of Economic Thought*, his memoirs *Crowded Hours*, and *Where Did We Go Wrong?*

AMARTYA SEN is Master of Trinity College, Cambridge, and a Professor Emeritus at Harvard University. He is a development economist whose academic work has largely been concerned with the world's poorest people. He was awarded a Nobel Prize in 1998 for his contributions to welfare economics.

ARTHUR M. SCHLESINGER, JR. is a writer, historian, and twice winner of the Pulitzer Prize: for History in 1946, and for Biography in 1966. He was Special Assistant to President Kennedy (1961–1963) and president of the Academy of Arts and Letters (1981–1984). He is a former professor at Harvard University and the City University of New York.

STUART CARY WELCH is Curator Emeritus, Department of Islamic and Later Indian Art, the Harvard University Art Museums.

ANDREA WILLIAMS has worked as John Kenneth Galbraith's editor and personal assistant for almost forty years. She is the associate editor of this collection.

The Editor

HELEN SASSON has had an extensive career running her group of companies in information-based areas, including industrial market research, conference organization, and book publishing. She is editor of *LSE on Social Science* and a member of the board of the London School of Economics.

ON GALBRAITH THE PERSON,

EVENTS IN HIS LIFE, AND

THEIR INFLUENCES

ON HIS IDEAS

A QUIXOTE
OF THE PLAINS

———◆———

Carlos Fuentes

Dᴜʀɪɴɢ ᴛʜᴇ ꜰᴜɴᴇʀᴀʟ of President John F. Kennedy, foreign dignitaries as well as North American personalities assembled in one of the White House reception rooms. Two profiles swam over the sea of heads: those of the French President General Charles de Gaulle, and of the Harvard Professor John Kenneth Galbraith. At a given moment, de Gaulle had Galbraith summoned to him.

"I was struck by the fact that there is a man taller than I," de Gaulle (six feet six in height) imperially told Galbraith (almost seven feet tall).

"What distinguishes us from the rest of humanity?" the President of France went on.

"First," Galbraith drawled, "we are more noticeable than others, as you have just proven. And second, we must always be more virtuous than others, since everyone can see us and we cannot hide."

"Very good, very good," De Gaulle smiled. "But don't forget to be implacable to other men of lesser height."

Nevertheless, every Frenchman carries a Napoleon hidden in his bosom, just as each of Bonaparte's soldiers carried a marshal's baton in his knapsack. Galbraith, a son of the generous Canadian plains, hides nothing. His height is but the vertical form of his straightforwardness, his horizontal plainness, in the Spanish sense of *ilaneza*, openness, frankness, even if it gives him the right—Galbraith, straight as an arrow —to look down on the world's follies, which only he can see from such a vantage point, with a very dry irony. The important thing, nevertheless, is that Galbraith's mind is even taller than he, yet it is not in the clouds. His thoughts always touch the ground. This Antheus of Anglo-American social democracy (what the gringos call "liberalism") is the Quixote of economics. Watch him, lance in arm, undo reactionary torts, a paladin who unmasks the most pious conservative illusions, revealing, behind the noble demeanor of right-wing barons, the greedy countenance of the grubbiest usurer.

Thanks to Galbraith, we know that the much-decried State intervention in the economy is nothing compared with the permanent intervention of the giant corporations. Galbraith unveils the theater of the economic world, and we see conservative governments proclaiming the supremacy of market forces in everything except two matters: bailing out the corporations and augmenting defense spending, which continue to be the State's unrenounceable mission for the benefit of private enterprise, a matter far too serious to be left to the whimsical hand of God. No self-respecting private corporation, says Galbraith, would ever abandon itself to the capricious tides of the marketplace.

In a photograph I have of him, my son, Carlos, surprised Ken at the door of his bedroom during one of our visits to his house in Cambridge, where we invariably enjoy the great hospitality of Galbraith and his beautiful, fragile wife, Kitty. The professor's kimono accentuates his pencil-like figure, his personal calligraphy, and his fidelity toward the Orient. Moments later he will ensconce himself in his study to write for six uninterrupted hours, reminding us all that the end of communism nowhere assures the triumph of social justice and that the subject of the economist is no less than concrete human beings, their well-being, their health, their education, their hope. No absolutism, no statistic, no abstract chart, should deflect us from these ends, so modest, yet so forgotten by economists, but not, says Galbraith, by common citizens who, contrary to economists, have not been trained to invent illusions.

I look up at Galbraith's great height and ask myself, What would we do without him? — before anticipating myself, How much we will always need him!

THE AMBASSADORS GALBRAITH:
DIPLOMATIC LESSONS
FROM MY FATHER

◆

Peter Galbraith

IN 1961, President Kennedy appointed John Kenneth Galbraith United States Ambassador to India. I was ten years old and did not want to go. I had my friends and pets, and was wary of exchanging a not particularly happy school environment in Cambridge for an uncertain one far away. There was no question of my not going, but my father pretended it was a matter for negotiation. I was unpersuaded.

Then, on March 29, I came home from school to find a special delivery letter addressed to me, bearing the White House as the return address. The President had written to me of India's attractions and the possibilities of an animal menagerie far more exotic than that of Cambridge. He compared my situation with that of his younger siblings, who were anxious about being uprooted to London when Joseph P. Kennedy became Ambassador to the Court of St. James's. The President appealed to my incipient sense of public service, saying that he considered the children of his appointees overseas to be his junior Peace Corps, charged with "helping your parents do a good job for our country." The letter was signed John F. Kennedy, with a postscript, handwritten with a ballpoint pen: "I wish I were going also."

The letter's arrival leaked to the Boston press, and for several days I was a local media star, appearing on television and in the local papers. I was also trapped. Now I had to go to India. More recently I have come to suspect that Ken Galbraith wrote the letter himself, and that Kennedy, impressed with its grace, had added the postscript. In any event, by arranging for the letter, my father scored an early diplomatic triumph. I went to India and acquired two horses, two deer, peacocks, parrots, a dog, a Siamese cat (whose naming caused a diplomatic incident, as my father has frequently told), and a leopard cub, which was returned to the zoo after trying to maul my mother.

Thirty-two years later, in 1993, I was appointed United States Ambassador to Croatia. My father admirably restrained his instinct to instruct. He offered only one piece of advice: control your communications. In New Delhi, he insisted that all messages go through him, especially those from the CIA station. When funny business brewed, he was able to stop it.

The advice was sound but, in an era of computers, classified e-mail, and secure telephones, practically impossible to implement. I learned from the press (nothing is kept secret in Washington) that my station chief believed I was insufficiently anti-Iranian, and had devoted considerable energy reporting to his headquarters on me and others in the embassy. As a result, I spent several uncomfortable months explaining to congressional investigators that I was not part of an international Shi'ite conspiracy.

Even though my father demurred on further instruction, I had already absorbed lessons from his dining room table stories, his writings, and my own memories as a pre-teen in India. He did not think being an ambassador required much work. During his twenty-nine months in India, he wrote four books: *The McLandress Dimension, The Scotch, Ambassador's Journal,* and his most recent publication, *Letters to President Kennedy.*[1] Further, as the Kennedy letters reveal, he was extensively engaged with the administration on non-India matters, including economic policy and Indochina.

Ideally, an ambassador wants to control policy toward the country to which he is accredited. Galbraith's ambitions went further. He wanted a role in the major foreign policy questions of the administration. Being abroad risks being forgotten, and, indeed, surprisingly few envoys (career or political) successfully set the agenda for the country to which they are accredited, much less deal with larger issues. Setting policy requires three main elements: (1) knowing what you want to do; (2) being able to communicate your views cogently and briefly; and (3) developing allies in Washington who will advance your cause.

Ken Galbraith both knew the policies he wanted and how to advocate them persuasively. He is fond of saying that the Kennedy letters are the best writing he ever did, even though it was for an audience of one. A single dull letter, and no others would be read. The letters are as literary ("When I wake up at night I worry that in our first year in office we will be credited with losing Laos, which we did not have, losing East Berlin, which we did not have, and [touchy point] with failing to persuade the world that Formosa is China") as they are bureaucratically skillful. Galbraith's messages were read and

---

1. For one year of my tour I kept a detailed daily record of my diplomatic activities. Eventually it was subpoenaed by a congressional committee. Few in government today keep diaries, and any form of written candor involves peril.

discussed. Secretary Rusk paid them an unintended compliment when he demanded that Galbraith be instructed to send his messages through the State Department. When asked by Kennedy about this, Galbraith replied that communicating through the State Department was like fornicating through a mattress. The answer surely enchanted Kennedy and kept the direct channel open. (Like all subsequent ambassadors, I was firmly instructed to send no message directly to the White House unless personally asked to do so by the President.)

It is remarkable how good and prescient Galbraith's substantive policy recommendations were. From 1961 on, he was unstinting in his objections to United States military involvement in Indochina. He predicted that the South Vietnamese would gladly let American soldiers do the fighting for them, and that military involvement was certain to be more politically damaging to the Democrats than a South Vietnamese defeat. He belittled the Pentagon's domino theory (in which Saigon's fall would knock over other Asian dominoes, leading to a communist conquest of the continent). Galbraith observed that he could see little difference between a communist jungle and a capitalist one.

He recommended a Berlin strategy based on recognition of East Germany while maintaining a commitment to eventual German unity. Heresy in 1961, this policy was adopted in 1971 and contributed to German unification in 1989. He advocated a China policy that entailed recognition for Peking, while trying to preserve a seat for Taiwan in the UN General Assembly. This bargain was attainable in 1961, and Taipei would have had a far better deal than it got ten years later. The day before he departed for India, he got word of the impending Bay of Pigs invasion and sent Kennedy a strong warning against "adventurism which counts (or assumes) the gains of some particular operation or enterprise or coup but does not count the larger costs either of success or failure." The message was oblique, referring to the Caribbean rather than Cuba, since Galbraith was not supposed to know of the operation. Galbraith's complaints against atmospheric nuclear testing saw a far happier policy outcome with the 1963 Limited Test Ban Treaty.

Galbraith's commonsense approach was decisive in the biggest crisis of his tenure: the October–November 1962 Sino-Indian war. In his diary, he noted the absence of a State Department response to the crisis: "For a week, I have had a considerable war on my hands without a single telegram, letter, telephone call, or other communication of guidance." (I had many such weeks in the Balkans.) This did not unduly disturb him. He decided what needed to be done and then informed the Department. "I got back to the Department with a statement of our policy. It is far safer to propose a course of action to the Department and ask for confirmation than to wait for the latter's instructions, which may never arrive or be inconvenient," he observed. (Often finding myself without guidance during the Balkans war, I frequently followed my father's approach. I was supported enthusiastically by my desk officers, who on several occasions helped persuade higher-ups to ratify my actions. Still, I would have felt more comfortable with the President as my personal ally.)

From the start, Galbraith saw the Chinese military movements in the high Himalayas as a border dispute and not a prelude to a larger military campaign. Because these hostilities coincided with the Cuban missile crisis, there were many who would have willingly seen the Chinese actions as an element in the broader international communist conspiracy. Not only was Washington inattentive to the conflict, the Indian government responded with panic. For a time, Ken Galbraith not only formulated the United States response (a policy that included strong support for India's territorial position and modest United States arms assistance), but also helped guide the Indians out of their disarray.

In his writings, Ken Galbraith harshly criticizes the State Department. In *Ambassador's Journal*, he dreams of it burning down and of the headline NO SURVIVORS. To Kennedy, he wrote of how sensible decisions from the political level are translated into cabled instructions from "what by some witticism is called the working level." And in 1968, he published a novel, *The Triumph*, that parodied State Department policy-making. (In the novel, a Somoza-style dictator of a fictional Central American republic—its capital full of Venetian-style architecture, since the book was written in the Gritti Palace—is replaced by a moderate reformer. The reformer proves too dangerous to the ambassador and the assistant secretary, who arrange a countercoup, in which the departed dictator's American-educated son comes to power. The State Department does not know that the son had fallen under the sway of his Marxist professors at the University of Michigan.)

The State Department today is a much better institution. Ken Galbraith served in an institution dominated by white men, many of whom were the products of prep schools and Ivy League universities. Some were good, but many were only serving their time. Galbraith found it a lazy institution, occupied with endless meetings and far too many people. Not surprisingly, he found that this combination made for decisions by the lowest common denominator and policy stasis. Today, the Foreign Service is much more diverse, drawn from all over the country, and with growing numbers of women in all ranks. (It has been far less successful in recruiting African Americans.) The number of Foreign Service officers is fewer than in the 1960s, in spite of a vastly greater United States diplomatic presence. I found the Foreign Service officers who worked for me in Zagreb, and with me in Washington, to be hard-working, creative, and deeply committed to progressive goals, including human rights and international justice. In the Balkans, they took personal risks that the military would not allow servicemen to take, and it is no coincidence that most of the Americans who died during the recent war and peace implementation were on diplomatic missions. I felt fortunate to work with this team rather than one from my father's era.

As long as I have known him, my father has had strongly held views that he has rarely been reticent to express. This is not thought to be a conventional trait for a diplomat, but it served Ken Galbraith well. Contemporary American diplomats are less reticent and more forceful, mostly to good effect, in my experience.

Still, at the core of democratic discourse is tolerance; to be able to disagree on policy and still be civil. Galbraith is not only civil but able to maintain close personal relations with his policy adversaries, both domestic and foreign. How else to explain his friendships with the Russian economist Stanislav Menshikov, who used to be a communist, and the American writer William F. Buckley, Jr., who used to be a conservative? Perhaps he believes civility can contribute to redemption, as is clearly demonstrated in the aforementioned examples.

Naturally, I tried to preach and practice this Galbraithian approach to disagreement in the former Yugoslavia. It was an uphill battle in a culture where holding different political views equates with being an enemy.

Those who know Galbraith well know he is not universally forgiving. Enduring objects of his distaste include Secretary of State Dean Rusk and Assistant Secretary of State Philips Talbot. For him, they embodied a foreign policy establishment that, out of cowardice and laziness, accepted in full the given truths (or conventional wisdom) of the Cold War. The foreign policy elite tagged those who did not conform as unpatriotic, weak, or unprofessional. Thus, those who argued against alarmist assessments of Soviet ambition or prowess were naïve; those who opposed Vietnam unpatriotic; those who favored normal relations with Communist China unrealistic. Being right made little difference. The only foreign policy professionals to suffer for Vietnam were those who opposed the war. Indeed, the opposition to Tony Lake's nomination in 1997 was almost certainly payback for his Vietnam-related resignation twenty-seven years earlier. Of course, no one has yet to challenge the professionalism of those who made wildly wrong assessments of the Soviet Union's military and economic strength and, accordingly, missed the factors that led to the country's demise.

As with the State Department, the foreign policy establishment is less male and more inclusive than in the 1960s. Still, there are enormous pressures for conformity. In the late 1980s, I worked extensively on Iraq, and, unlike other Middle East experts, I traveled widely in the country, observing the Saddam Hussein regime in action at home. I came to oppose strongly the widely applauded Reagan-Bush policy of reaching out to Saddam Hussein, on the grounds that a regime that gassed its own people (the Kurds) and attacked its neighbor (Iran) was not likely to be a force for stability in the Persian Gulf. Even after the invasion of Kuwait, the Iraq fraternity (all of whom had been wrong) continued to argue that my views were not professional, having been unduly influenced by human rights considerations.

My lawyer brother Alan says that no major figure in public

life ever made as good use of the First Amendment as our father. As an ambassador and, later, as the leading opponent of United States involvement in Vietnam, he was fearless of the consequences to his reputation, career, or person. He was never reckless, taking care to prepare well his arguments and present them calmly. But he did not hesitate to say and do what he believed.

I served as ambassador through Europe's biggest war in fifty years. I did not always agree with my government's policy, particularly at the beginning of the war, when we were not as engaged as we later became. My views were often not welcome, but I advanced them: carefully prepared, as well written as possible, forcefully, and repeatedly. Consciously or not, I was imitating my father's approach. I do not know whether I served my career well or poorly. I left Croatia feeling good about my work there and proud of my contribution to ending a war.

After nineteen years of government service I am convinced that the greatest and most common vice of politicians and bureaucrats is cowardice. John Kenneth Galbraith is the most courageous man I have known. As much as his intelligence and graceful writing, this courage is the reason for his extraordinary influence on our times.

GALBRAITH AS A

NEIGHBOR

◆

Daniel Patrick Moynihan

It was a dark and stormy day: November 23, 1992. Peter Galbraith, then a member of the Senate Foreign Relations Committee staff, and I had finally reached the center of Sarajevo. We were, properly speaking, a CODEL, short for "Congressional Delegation," on a scheduled visit to the besieged capital. The air force was to have got us there, but in midflight from Frankfurt the pilot received orders from SECDEF (let the reader decipher) that the mission was off: DIVERT TO ZAGREB. The next morning, however, we were aboard a Canadian C-130 flying in food to Bosnia's capital. The city then had one day's supply, and the Canadians (and others) were determined that the citizens not starve. The radar was down; the shelling getting closer to the airstrip; the cloud cover rising, then falling. But they made it, and there we were.

At the airport, that is. Next came a ride in the belly of a Ukrainian armored personnel carrier. Much machine-gunning. Quick shift to an Egyptian APC, and off to the Prime Minister's residence; that is to say, Ali Itzetbegovic, the Islamic leader of what in time would become a third of his country.

The Prime Minister's staff did their best to make our arrival something of an occasion; we were, I believe, the first Americans there since the civil conflict had begun. We were escorted to an official reception room. Some television was there, but the power gave out almost immediately. Not to worry. The Prime Minister sat us down; asked if Peter was by chance related to the world-famous economist John Kenneth Galbraith. Indeed he was. How splendid, our host declared, whereupon our conversation turned to agricultural economics, the causes of great economic depressions, the concept of a mixed economy. It went on and on, until dusk fell and the shelling got heavier and closer. The Egyptians sent word that they were heading back to base. And so we departed, with scarcely a word about civil war or, if you prefer, Serbian aggression.

Which, however, seemed perfectly normal. In the presence of a Galbraith, even one of the next generation, you talked about ideas. The more, the better; the more contrarian, the more welcome. I so attest. For years we were neighbors on Francis Avenue, named for an early Harvard College carpenter, which proceeds from the Yard toward the Somerville border, hooking about to end at Norton's Woods, of which e. e. cummings wrote (and now the grounds of the American Academy of Arts and Sciences). It was for practical purposes an extension of Harvard Yard itself; Francis's own neoclassical house at one end, the more modest dwellings of Daniel Bell and Simon Kuznets at the other. In between were splendid houses of great professors, none more than Number 30, where the Galbraiths lived. (We lived a few doors farther on.)

Make that "where the Galbraiths entertained." Continuously. He wrote or lectured in the morning. Next came lunch, which the incomparable Kitty would have arranged, conversation in mind, for which the essential ingredient was variety. Hence the guests. A graduate student, a don, some visiting Indians, members of an undergraduate seminar, someone with the latest news from Washington. There was no doctrine, no givens; indeed, there was a general air of the futility of seeking certainty in political environments. Lunch would go on until tea, followed by cocktails, dinner, brandy, the participants in the colloquy continuously overlapping, making new friends, hearing new ideas. Through it all Himself presided from a great corner chair, feet up, with close attention and unfailing good humor. (Although I once felt a measure of anguish over his response to an Indian graduate student who suggested that his host was an instrument of American imperialism.)

No visitor from the political world (Liz and I were something such) could fail to note the political dimension of the gatherings. High politics: what should governments do. This was the man; the world was his subject. It fell to me to review his wondrous autobiography *A Life in Our Times* (1981) for *The New Yorker*. I began the review on just this note, thinking he would like it:

> John Kenneth Galbraith is one of a long succession of immigrants who have made their way in America through services to a political party and to political party leaders.

Indeed, he records that when he joined the Department of Agriculture in 1934:

> [it was] immediately suggested that I go on the payroll . . . I as promptly agreed. I was not a citizen, but it is not certain that one was even asked about such details in those civilized days . . . I was, however, required to go to a small room on the upper floor and meet the President's representative, James A. Farley, the Postmaster General and custodian of Democratic patronage. There I affirmed that I was a Democrat . . . My salary was at the rate of $3200 a year . . . Not since have I been short of money.

Nor short of the desire to give it away in as many modes and amounts as only an economist could master.

His greatest feat in politics is probably the least known. During World War II, in the very opposite of the Keynesian stereotype, Galbraith and a few others in the Office of Price Administration actually produced a decline in prices during wartime — the classic setting for inflation. Inflation dropped from 9.7 percent in 1941 to 2.1 percent in 1944. Writing books is one thing; running an economy launched on a world war is something else. Here is a man who could do both. And be a neighbor, to boot. On the morning after it was reported that I was to go off to India as President Nixon's ambassador, our doorbell rang. There were the Ambassador and Kitty, with garlands to welcome us, at whatever distance, to India. The weeks that followed seemed like one long seminar and total immersion in a lending library, as he would fetch two- and three-volume histories from his library for me to take with me. (And never a word about the President, who was not exactly his favorite.)

This was a lifelong practice. Jawaharlal Nehru once complained to Averell Harriman that Galbraith was forever sending him books. "But," Harriman replied, "he is after all an author." "I realize that," said Nehru. "But these are other people's books!"

Very well. Find another Harvard professor who sends out other people's books!

There has not been one like him in our time. Not least because, with some celebrated exceptions, he liked us all without limit, and it showed.

A VERY PERSONAL
BIRTHDAY TRIBUTE

◆

Eric Roll

O<small>N THE</small> 15<small>TH OF</small> O<small>CTOBER</small> 1998, Ken will be ninety, following me by about ten months in reaching that landmark age. I mention this fact because for two thirds of this long life span, we have known each other, been very close friends, and had the unusual luck of being able to keep in touch throughout the period across continents and oceans in many different locations and in many different circumstances.

I first met Ken Galbraith just after Christmas 1939, in Philadelphia, at the annual meeting of the American Economic Association. I was in the United States as a Rockefeller Fellow, and my first port of call was Harvard. From Harvard we went with several other people to Philadelphia, where we met Ken. He himself had just left Harvard to become an assistant professor at Princeton. John Kenneth Galbraith was, of course, on my list of people I had to get to know as soon as possible, and this first encounter in Philadelphia brought that about. At Harvard, Ken had belonged to that remarkable group of young economists and other academics in the social sciences, including some at the Massachusetts Institute of Technology and other universities in and around

Cambridge, who had marked forever the flowering of the inquiring mind in the social circumstances of our time.

Many of that brilliant group were to demonstrate the definite achievement of supremacy by American economic science in the Western world. American economics had already drawn alongside British economics some fifty years earlier, but by the late thirties, the time I am talking about—and with the towering exception of Keynes—there was no doubt that the United States had become the center of economic inquiry. Paul Samuelson, at that time a junior fellow at Harvard, having come from Chicago and, before very long, to win the Nobel Prize in Economics, was an outstanding example of that brilliant group. He could probably be described as the leading mainstream economist of this century. Many others of a rather more radical description, of whom Ken Galbraith could be counted a member, were to provide continuing and increasing intellectual additions to the practical ideas generated by the New Deal, which were quite active. Some of these "left-wing" scholars wrote a remarkable little book that left a permanent imprint on subsequent generations. This was *An Economic Program for American Democracy* (New York, Vanguard Press, 1938). Among its authors were John Wilson, Paul Sweezy, Dick Gilbert, Arthur Stuart, and Lorie Tarshis.

I was very anxious to get to know Ken well, and the opportunity for this came in the early months of 1940, during my fairly peripatetic sojourn in the United States, when I went to our second university in the United States, namely, Princeton. My wife and I met him and Kitty again and soon became close friends. They were responsible for finding us our first apartment in Princeton, and, although my main academic location at the time was at Princeton's Institute for Advanced Study, while Ken was at the university, I managed to see a great deal of him.

Ken was known primarily as an agricultural economist, although even then that was far too narrow a description both of his interests and of his intellectual range. He was—and those who got to know him much later in life may find this rather difficult to believe—a somewhat taciturn person. The conversation in the Galbraith household, particularly when it came to more general topics of the day, had to be carried mainly by Kitty. It was at a much later stage that Ken became more fluent. His renown rested not so much on his written work, of which at that time there was relatively little, but rather on his reputation among his peers, that very remarkable group, as I said, of outstanding economists on the eastern seaboard. It had already penetrated to some extent beyond the boundaries of the United States, and certainly in the U.K., particularly in Cambridge, the name of Galbraith was well known.

The intellectual and political climate in which we met was one in which the New Deal was still very much alive, although it was beginning to be overshadowed by threats of war, which had just then broken out in Europe. This was for some time known as the phase of the "phony war."

The conversation of the young economists among whom I moved, including, of course, Ken, still centered on the state of the American economy. The United States had already demonstrated the achievements of the New Deal in overcoming the sequelae of the Depression. The conversation also turned on the difficulties, economic and also social and political, that Europe was experiencing and that many recognized were really at the root of the growth of fascism and Nazism and, therefore, of the threat of war that overhung everything.

American public opinion at large, although broadly sympathetic to the Allies, was still isolationist or at least neutralist. It was also plagued, although happily only at the periphery, by the America First movement, which, under the guise of neutralism and isolationism, was, in fact, dominated by elements friendly to the Nazis. Among the group of young economists and social and political scientists to which Ken belonged, there was, of course, no question of not totally supporting the democratic countries in Europe. It started somewhat feebly, and this was partly the consequence of the appeasement policy in Britain and France. But quite soon it began to summon up resistance to Hitler and to the Italian Fascists. Nevertheless, it is only fair to say that in the more left-wing elements the old hesitation and even resistance to American involvement in war, tinged with a pacifist element, was contending with the drive toward active support for the Allied cause. American participation was, therefore, still controversial. Lend-Lease, the first positive move of the Roosevelt Administration, was strongly supported by all of the young intellectuals, and when the situation became really critical, there was no doubt that the vast majority of these younger elements were strongly in support of American participation in the war.

Many of them were drawn into the war machine as their counterparts in the United Kingdom had been. Ken, for example, soon found himself in Washington, involved in the machinery for price control and the maintenance of civilian supplies by one means or another, including rationing.

I too found myself in Washington, working in the British Food Mission,[2] and that enabled us to keep closely in touch during the war in our respective areas of activity, in addition to all the other interests we had in common. Soon Ken reached a commanding position in the Office of Price Administration and Civilian Supplies, as it was first called. He

2. This was in spring 1941, when the Lend-Lease Act was passed.

was joined there by many of the people both he and I knew from the universities, who were called upon to apply their economic analysis and their knowledge of the more applied branches of economics to the task of running the administrative and legislative controls of the American economy that the war had made necessary.

I think this period, together with a later one I shall presently mention, had a tremendous effect on the development of Ken's character and his *modus operandi* and general attitude to the world. He had never been an Ivory Tower economist, and his earlier concern with agricultural economics was typical of his inclination to be interested primarily in resolving problems of applied economics, or at any rate of economics in the sense of practical improvements of the operation of the economy and of its effect on the welfare of the citizens.

This period in Washington in price administration added to Ken's equipment a very large amount of knowledge both of the problems and of practical ways of resolving them, as well as a knowledge of the business world. This seems to me a particularly important aspect. Without ever losing sight of the public policy objectives he was called upon to achieve, he acquired a good deal of realism about the way in which the business world actually worked and the manner in which people in business were motivated. This, therefore, gave him a much sharper, much more discriminating approach to the good and the bad sides of the economy and of that part of humanity which was directly active in it. His sort of amused and slightly skeptical, not to say cynical, attitude to the business world and to what really moves it, as well as his ability to distinguish carefully between real motives and pretense, were developed during that phase and have remained with him ever since. This period and the constant contact both within the administration as well as with its clients—that is, in business as well as in sections of the community that needed to be consulted in regard to the effects of wartime developments, such as scarcities and price rises—also gave Ken a much broader view of the world. All his subsequent work and writings show very clearly that new insight. His work is completely in contrast with that of others of his generation of economists who developed in a model-building, mathematic, formula-seeking direction. Kenneth showed throughout his subsequent writing a knowledge of the real world that is too often absent from the writing of his contemporaries. He also became much more fluent, much more able to express himself. Indeed, he developed a distinctive and attractive style in his public speaking that was both effective and aesthetic. For many years thereafter he was a much sought-after public speaker in all kinds of circumstances and environments.

Although totally free from that sometimes almost subservient attitude that some Americans have toward the British, he had a great deal of sympathy and respect for Britain, and particularly for those who were of a similar way of thinking and for the many distinguished economists, especially at Cambridge, whom he got to know in later years.

When he left the public service, he passed another important landmark in his development. That was when he became an editor of *Fortune* magazine. This strengthened and enlarged his concern with the real world in an even more direct way than contact with public affairs through government administration had provided. He became an extremely fluent writer, a quality that journalistic exigencies had fostered in him. From that time onward, I think, he always believed that he had to write something every day. When he had a book under construction, he never failed to add something, even if it was only one page every morning. He could write fluidly and with a newly developed style that combined the high academic tradition with the best forms of magazine journalism, of which there were some outstanding examples to be found in the United States at that time.

When back teaching at Harvard and continuing with research and writing books and articles, he maintained his contacts with the political circles in Washington, of course with the Democratic Party, and more particularly with the more advanced, not to say left-wing, segments of that party. When the Kennedy Administration arrived, there was much speculation about what particular part Ken would play, until it was finally decided by the President to send him to India as ambassador, at that time thought to be a somewhat unexpected role for him. However, even while ambassador in New Delhi, he continued to keep in close touch with the White House and to offer advice on many other matters. Once again this new phase of his activities provided the opportunity for still further development and enlargement of his grasp of affairs, of his interest in them, and of his ability to write and to speak. The embassy in New Delhi, particularly in those relatively early days of Indian independence and the presence of some of the giants of Indian politics, gave him an entirely new dimension, not only in diplomacy but also in the problems of a developing economy under a democratic regime. He formed close friendships with Nehru and other leaders of India, and also, together with his wife, Kitty, developed a remarkable interest in Indian art. He started a collection of Indian miniatures, a subject on which he became both an expert and a great amateur.

On his return from diplomatic service, Ken became what in fact he has been since and what he is now. He continued to write books and articles, he continued to speak in different parts of the world, frequently visiting Europe, particularly both England and France, and was, more generally, a point of contact either in Cambridge or in his country house in Vermont, or wherever he happened to be, for anyone seeking advice, good conversation, exchange of views on matters ranging from art, literature, and cultural aspects generally to current politics everywhere in the world.

Despite the enormous volume of his literary output, I do not propose to say much about his books here, as these will no doubt be dealt with by other contributors to this volume. Nearly all have been best-sellers. And some have remained classics from their first appearance to this day, notably *The Affluent Society*. Much of what he wrote in that book is even truer today than it was then, although today the outstanding gap is that between private affluence and public poverty.

This has become even more marked (and would deserve another book) in a country in which the millionaires are now counted in the hundreds of thousands and even the billionaires in the hundreds.

One fairly recent book is particularly noteworthy: a concise, broad-brush, but highly perceptive review of the development of economics. Perhaps even more rewarding than the individual books are his collections of essays, partly because they show the extraordinary variety of his interests and knowledge and partly because they reveal, even more than the major volumes, his relaxed, amused, and gently satirical approach to the world's follies. One aspect of his writing particularly deserves to be mentioned in this context, and that is his affinity to Thorstein Veblen, about whom he has written. Veblen too was a great critic of society and a coiner of memorable phrases; and there are clear similarities between the Minnesota Scandinavian and the Cambridge-Canadian Scot. However, the former's criticism is often dour and tinged with a certain bitterness, while the latter's is almost invariably cheerful.

◆ ◆ ◆

I have concentrated in what I have written on Ken's development from the time I first knew him to the present day. I would like now to say something by way of a general assessment of his position. This is not easy. As an economist, Ken, as I have already indicated, is somewhat apart from the mainstream of those economists properly so-called who are still very much influenced by Keynes (now split into unreconstructed, reconstructed, post- and past-Keynesians), as well as from the more fashionable schools. These include behaviorist economists, rational expectation economists, modelbuilders, formula-seekers, who express themselves almost entirely in mathematical symbols. Ken is, I suppose, closest to the mainstream economists of the kind still flourishing in both of the Cambridge communities. But he is more than that. He is a broadly based social scientist and social critic. He has written on political power; he has written on administration; he has written on practical economic problems as well as the practicalities of politics. He cannot, therefore, be classified with the common run of economists, sociologists, and political scientists. All those who have hoped (and indeed done something toward it) that he would be the recipient of the Nobel Prize must be disappointed, precisely because he does not fit into what has become the modern mold. For—unfortunately—those who are responsible for awarding the Nobel Prize have gone more and more into areas they regard as "scientific"—though I would often call them pseudo-scientific. They have very little to do with that broad tradition of economics as it developed almost two hundred years ago and has been carried on by the greatest spirits of the science throughout this period and to the present day. In fact, had the Nobel Prize Committee taken a broader view of its mandate, Ken would obviously have been a very suitable and very eminent laureate.

His fame, nevertheless, is not diminished by the absence of

this particular accolade; I might mention, incidentally, that he has received many others from many different countries. His fame rests firmly on his inspiration of what continues to be best in the social sciences and, more particularly, in economics, what Bacon called the "tendency to use," that is to say, a practical purpose, namely, to better the condition of mankind. Ken has undoubtedly done a great deal toward that; when the opportunity offered, he has done so in practical terms, as he did during the war and during his ambassadorship in India. But when there was no practical opportunity, he certainly has done it by intellectual endeavor, by his writing, by his speaking, and by his availability as an adviser to all those who seek enlightenment.

I would add to this, if I may, that he has also been a most staunch and most rewarding friend to many, not least to the writer of these pages.

GALBRAITH AND

POLITICS

———————◆———————

Arthur M. Schlesinger, Jr.

Political economy was the original term. Adam Smith used it, and so did John Stuart Mill. The more antiseptic term "economics" took over in the last quarter of the nineteenth century. Like "mathematics" and "aesthetics," it seemed somehow more scientific. In recent years "political econ-omy" has made a mild comeback, and happily so. Economics, after all, is the science, or art (or roulette wheel), of choice, and therefore has the keenest possible bearing on public policy.

So at any rate John Kenneth Galbraith has always conceived it. Theory in his view is not an end in itself. Its function, he has always supposed, is to explain, illuminate, and, if possible, improve the conditions of life. Politics and government in this perspective are not digressions for economists but are central to their work.

Galbraith himself has been immersed in politics almost from the cradle. His father was a local leader in the Liberal Party of Ontario. A tall man, he instructed his son, who promised to be even taller, that (as Galbraith recalled in *The Scotch*) "we were obliged because of our enormous size to alter the world to our specifications." From an early age the son accompanied the father to Liberal Party meetings. In later years Galbraith liked to tell how his father, mounting a manure pile to address a farm audience, apologized for speaking from the Tory platform. When congratulated on the brilliance of the sally, the father replied realistically, "It was good, but it didn't change any votes."

After attending the Ontario Agricultural College, Galbraith crossed the border to do agricultural economics at the University of California. This was in 1930. For a time, politics was subordinated to economic education. He read Marshall and was indoctrinated in the neoclassical tradition. He also read Veblen, a more abiding influence.

Galbraith found Veblen "dangerously attractive." A Norwegian from rural Minnesota, Veblen looked on both classical economics and academic folkways with an elaborately ironic eye, which the Canadian from rural Ontario found highly congenial. Veblen's anthropological perspective on economic behavior seemed richer than the oversimplified motivation of the neoclassical "economic man." And, as Galbraith later put it, "along with all else, Veblen was an engaging, wonderfully amusing writer." From Veblen, Galbraith not only took a fascination with the whiplash phrase but gained a recognition of the social context of economic behavior and an institutionalist bias to balance Marshall's equilibrium model.

Neither Marshall nor Veblen encouraged interest in political economy—Marshall, because he feared that an intrusive state would disrupt the workings of the market; Veblen, because he was incurably pessimistic about the possibilities of liberal reform. Veblenian institutionalism, with its dream of a "soviet of engineers," prompted utopian expectations, in some distant day, of technocratic planning (Howard Scott, the prophet of Technocracy during the Great Depression, was a follower of Veblen's) but had little or nothing to offer about government manipulation of economic levers in the interim.

Agricultural economics, however, nourished Galbraith's political interest. In 1930, farm households accounted for a quarter of the population of the United States. The free market had left agriculture a periodic disaster area. Productivity had grown at less than 1 percent a year in the first three decades of the century. Exclusion from the prosperity of the 1920s intensified the search for remedy. From the time of the Populists, farmers had looked to the national government for rescue. Agricultural economics was now in a state of creative ferment. Businessmen and economists were devising plans to stabilize farm prices, income, and production through one form or another of government intervention.

As a Canadian Liberal, Galbraith naturally identified with the Democrats in the United States. Frightened by the ever deeper Depression, the voters turned in 1932 to Franklin D. Roosevelt. The centerpieces of the early New Deal—the Agricultural Adjustment Administration and the National Recovery Administration—were the first peacetime experiments in national economic planning.

AAA was far more successful than NRA and carried forward the process that eventually transformed a weak, disorganized, and poverty-prone sector of the economy into a spectacular productive success. Watching agricultural recovery weakened Galbraith's faith in neoclassical economics. For it was the activist state—public technical assistance, public subsidies for research and development, public investment in education, in energy supply and in infrastructure, federal price stabilization, export promotion, credit and mortgage relief—that was saving the farmers. Under public ministration, agricultural productivity increased 5 percent annually—more than three times as fast as productivity among non-farm businesses. American farmers, today about 1 percent of the population, produce more than they did as 25 percent of the population in 1930.

Galbraith was twenty-five years old in 1934 when, still a Canadian citizen, he went to Washington and found a summer job in AAA, staying as a part-time consultant after he moved on to Harvard that autumn. In 1936 he boldly made speeches advocating Roosevelt's re-election. On reflection, he decided that, before he became more deeply involved in United States politics, he should regularize his status. In 1937, he became an American citizen. In the meantime, under the prodding of the liberal industrialist Henry Dennison and the stimulus of Keynes's *General Theory*, he began to expand his economic inquiries into the industrial sector.

A year at the University of Cambridge confirmed his Keynesianism. On his return to the United States, in 1938, he rejoined the New Deal, this time as a consultant to the National Resources Planning Board. Here, he studied the economic effects of federal public works expenditures. He had not, however, abandoned agricultural economics, and in 1940 became resident economist for the American Farm Bureau Federation in its Chicago headquarters. This may seem odd, because the Farm Bureau represented the big commercial producers and was the inveterate enemy of federal agencies, like the Farm Security Administration, concerned with rural poverty. But Galbraith agreed with the Farm Bureau on the virtue of high price supports for basic commodities, and he doubtless hoped to moderate the Farm Bureau's more extreme views on other matters. In any case, with his growing sense of the inevitability of economic concentration, he was skeptical of national belief in the sanctity of the family farm.

The outbreak of war in Europe brought Galbraith back to Washington in 1940 as deputy for the forceful New Deal economist Leon Henderson on the National Defense Advisory Commission. As Roosevelt's third-term election approached, he joined a small team commissioned to prepare campaign speech drafts for submission to FDR's top speechwriters Samuel Rosenman and Robert E. Sherwood. This was Galbraith's debut in what became in time a distinguished career as ghostwriter for presidential candidates. He was too far down the hierarchy in 1940, though, to influence the themes of the campaign. His team's most memorable contribution came from his friend Griffith Johnson, who originated the famous rhythmic triad of Martin, Barton, and Fish.

In April 1941, Henderson, now head of the Office of Price Administration, appointed Galbraith to take charge of price control. In the next two years Galbraith received political baptism by full immersion, often in extremely hot water. OPA, though popular among the people (at least according to the polls) and astonishingly successful in checking wartime inflation, was a major target for the right-wing press and for businessmen and farmers out to raise their prices, and, in consequence, a favored congressional scapegoat.

Henderson and Galbraith were irrepressible men, temperamentally ill-equipped to mollify opposition and especially deficient in the capacity to resist the temptation of a wisecrack. Galbraith's sallies, like his father's, were good but didn't change any votes; rather the contrary. After Republican gains in the 1942 midterm election, Henderson was thrown to the wolves. Trade publications demanded further sacrifices. *The Food Field Reporter,* the journal of the food trades, declared GALBRAITH MUST GO. Congressional committees took up the cry. In the spring of 1943, Galbraith followed Henderson to the wolves.

It was in this period that Galbraith and I first became friends. Up to that point we had managed to elude each other. He was at Cambridge University in 1938–1939, when I was in my last undergraduate year at Harvard. When I returned to Harvard in 1939, he had moved on to Princeton. At last we met in 1943. After OPA, Ken accepted odd government assignments while I was in the Office of Strategic Services, hoping to get overseas. We hit it off well from the start and discovered to our mutual pleasure that we were born on the same day—15 October—if not in the same year. This cheering coincidence is the strongest argument I know for astrology.

Soon Ken joined Henry Luce's *Fortune*, in those days a serious magazine analyzing the culture of corporations. Luce, though he disliked the New Deal, preferred good liberal writing to bad conservative writing, at least in *Fortune*. He was, Galbraith thought, a "superb editor . . . Luce's instruction in writing was a lifetime gift." Luce agreed. In 1960 he said to John F. Kennedy (who was greatly amused), "I taught Kenneth Galbraith to write. And I tell you, I've certainly regretted it."

Galbraith's literary style, up to now stolid and prosaic, in the manner of academic economists, was at last liberated to express exuberant wit and Veblenian irony. He was the first (thus far, the only) economist to be elected to the American Academy of Arts and Letters; from 1984 to 1987 he served as its president.

But Luce did not like his editors to become politically active, especially in the Democratic Party; so in 1944 Galbraith made no public speeches for FDR's fourth term. He did, however, participate in 1944–1945 in the U.S. Strategic Bombing Survey, and there our friendship resumed. In the spring of 1945, after the German surrender, I was in the OSS contingent in Wiesbaden while the USSBS team was established in baronial splendor in Bad Nauheim. From time to time Galbraith and his co-director, George Ball, would summon me for dinner. These instructive and highly convivial occasions consolidated a trilateral partnership that lasted over the next half century.

Back in the United States Ken and I were allied in 1947 in the founding of Americans for Democratic Action, a ginger group of New Dealers hoping to strengthen President Truman's liberal inclinations and at the same time preserve the liberal community against Stalinist penetration and manipulation.

In 1948, John D. Black, professor of agricultural economics at Harvard, invited Galbraith to join in a Harvard study of the marketing of farm products, with the academic rank of lecturer. The Economics Department soon proposed him for a permanent appointment. But members of the Board of Overseers, regarding Galbraith as a dangerous Keynesian, did their best to veto him. It finally took a threat of resignation in 1949 by James B. Conant, then President of Harvard, to overcome the opposition. During the angry controversy, Galbraith, advised to prove his dedication to teaching and scholarship, confined his support of Truman's reelection to the ballot box.

He now began the series of books that set forth his portrait of the contemporary economy. What is salient from the viewpoint of political economy is the skill with which Galbraith brought institutionalism to bear on public policy. A political leader could steep himself in Veblen, Simon Patten, John R. Commons, Wesley Mitchell, and other notable institutionalists without gaining much enlightenment about specific policy decisions: what to do about fiscal policy, monetary policy, exchange rates, the tariff, and so on. Only Adolf A. Berle and

Rexford Guy Tugwell in the institutionalist tradition bridged the gap to public policy; but one was a lawyer and the other a political scientist. Galbraith as a professional economist was especially qualified to unite institutionalism with dynamic equilibrium analysis; to marry, so to speak, Veblen and Keynes. The result was an institutionalist model that could deliver policy choices.

Like Patten and Berle, Galbraith regarded economic concentration as inevitable and, when properly controlled, beneficial. Monopoly and oligopoly were not, in his view, abnormal growths on the competitive market but rather the essence of the modern economy. The rise of the great corporation repealed Say's Law of Markets, the proposition that supply created its own demand, and destroyed the idea of a self-executing, self-regulating economy. Though Galbraith conceded a certain admonitory value to trust-busting rhetoric, he dismissed the antitrust dream of restoring laissez-faire competition as "the ultimate triumph of hope over experience." Nor, beyond a certain point, did he see government regulation as a reliable check on corporate power. The answer, he argued, lay in the countervailing power of other corporations, of trade unions, and, where private organization lagged, in government support for minimum wages and for farm prices.

American Capitalism (1952) pressed a sound point a little far. As Galbraith only briefly noted in the first edition, countervailing power would not control—indeed, might stimulate—a propensity to inflation. This omission he sought to repair in a second book of 1952, *A Theory of Price Control,* where he named inflation as "more than depression . . . the clear and present danger of our times and one that is potentially more destructive of the values and amenities of democratic life."

Nor, as he later noted, did countervailing power do much to help the unorganized—the rural and urban poor, the racial minorities, women, consumers—an omission repaired in *The Affluent Society* (1958). Here, he vividly contrasted the "social imbalance" between the opulence of private consumption and the starvation of public services.

A continuing theme was the role of power, a point, he contended, that had been systematically banished from conventional economics. "Economics divorced from consideration of the exercise of power is without meaning and certainly without relevance." Power relations in his view had displaced market relations in the modern economy, and he broadened his analysis to consider such questions as political power, military power, religious power, the power of ideas, even power between the sexes, the last giving much comfort to the women's liberation movement. He set forth his theory of power in *The Anatomy of Power* (1983), a work that has not received the attention it deserves either within or beyond the economics profession.

The Galbraith model emerged, I believe, from his observation of agriculture rescued from competitive drowning, as reinforced by his belief in the inevitability of economic concentration and by his experience with wartime controls. Unfortunately, the policy recommendations derived from the model ran afoul not only of the free-market theology of the Republicans but of the trust-busting, small-business, family-farm mythology of the Democrats, a set of clichés only temporarily shaken by the New Deal. Indeed, the apparent triumph of Keynesianism had produced the belief that the management of fiscal and monetary aggregates could solve economic problems without (apart from antitrust) any reorganization of economic structure.

The gap between what Galbraith thought should be done

and what even the more liberal of the two parties was prepared to consider became his perennial frustration in politics. This was evident when he returned to the political battles in 1952. George Ball and I persuaded him to come to Springfield, Illinois, in the late summer and work on speeches for the Democratic presidential candidate, Governor Adlai Stevenson of Illinois. Like all of us, he was simultaneously enchanted by Stevenson and dismayed by his Lake Forest reflexes on economic policy. With his persuasive air of authority, reinforced as always by his commanding height, Galbraith proved invaluable in moving the candidate to accept at least the New and Fair Deals.

Stevenson regarded Keynesianism with dark suspicion as the cause of budget deficits, but he was induced to keep his enthusiasm for budget-balancing out of his speeches. Nor did he like the planks in the Democratic platform most cherished by organized labor and by the farmers. The candidate finally consented to oppose the restrictive Taft-Hartley Labor Relations Act, though he insisted on the minor semantic victory of calling for its "replacement" rather than its "repeal." On farm policy, about which he knew or cared little, the candidate finally went along with "inflexible," now rebaptized "firm" by Galbraith, price supports. We all adored Stevenson and greatly enjoyed the campaign, if not the outcome, but concluded that our leader was in urgent need of instruction in modern economics.

This concern led in 1953 to the establishment of the so-called Finletter Group. Under the direction of Thomas K. Finletter, at once a former Secretary of the Air Force and a New York Reform Democrat, and with the help of Averell Harriman, soon to become Governor of New York, Galbraith, our beloved Harvard colleague Seymour Harris, and I arranged a series of seminars on issues of economic, social, and foreign policy. We were never sure that Stevenson ever read the position papers, nor was he faithful in his attendance.

Still, the process somewhat eroded Stevenson's commitment to economic orthodoxy. In the 1956 campaign he cheerfully expounded views that had gravely disturbed him four years earlier. The "experiment in adult education," as Galbraith called it, was deemed a success and led, after the 1956 defeat, to the establishment of the Democratic Advisory Council, with Galbraith as chairman of the domestic policy committee, and to the subsequent accumulation of policy capital for Kennedy's New Frontier.

The DAC made Galbraith a familiar figure in Democratic councils and cemented his relations with party leaders. He was closest to the junior senator from Massachusetts. Galbraith had known John F. Kennedy as an undergraduate at Harvard before the war. They became good friends in the 1950s. Galbraith liked Kennedy enormously. He saw him as less encumbered by vagrant orthodoxies than Stevenson, less deferential to received opinion, more open and direct of mind, more prepared to follow where reason led. He also saw him as more likely to beat Richard Nixon in 1960. On Kennedy's trips to Boston, the Galbraiths and Schlesingers would often join him for dinner in one of those dark-paneled private rooms at the famous old Boston restaurant Locke-Ober's. Galbraith became one of Kennedy's first declared supporters in the liberal community.

The growing affection was reciprocated. Kennedy delighted in Galbraith's company and valued his advice, on political as well as on economic matters. Like any serious politician, he subjected all advice to private discount, but he wanted Galbraith's, anyway. Agricultural policy was only the beginning: "I don't want to hear about agriculture from anyone but you, Ken. And I don't want to hear about it from you, either." He also admired Galbraith's capacity, notably lacking among the other liberals in his circle, to get along with men of affairs. Thus, when the time came for the obligatory mission to Bernard Baruch, Galbraith received the assignment and emerged with a pledge of support and an adequate campaign contribution.

Galbraith's political influence was at its height in the Kennedy years. Ever since a trip to India in 1956, he had harbored a desire to become ambassador to New Delhi; the wish was now fulfilled. Kennedy read Galbraith's cables with delight, followed his advice on relations with India, and asked him to take a look at other Asian matters, such as Vietnam. Here, the President, while rather sympathizing with Galbraith's advice, did not follow it. After Kennedy sent him to Saigon, Galbraith urged the pursuit of negotiations. Kennedy passed Galbraith's report to the Pentagon for comment. General Lyman Lemnitzer, chairman of the Joint Chiefs of Staff, righteously denounced the infamous idea of a "political solution." The American involvement deepened.

Though Galbraith sometimes suspected that Kennedy had dispatched him to India to minimize the administration's identification with his economic heresies, the President called him back often enough, on one occasion throwing a glittering White House party in his honor. On these visits Galbraith always found himself involved in whatever the current argument over economic policy was. He was the influential advocate of the first American peacetime experiment in income policy, the wage-price guideposts.

He won this fight, but lost a later one over the tax bill of 1963. The economy, everyone agreed, required fiscal stimulus; the question was whether stimulus should come through increased spending or reduced taxes. Galbraith argued with vigor that public services needed money more than the beneficiaries of tax reduction did. If tax reduction became the approved Keynesian remedy, it would increase the "social imbalance" between public and private goods and, by reducing appropriations, would hand conservatives a further weapon against affirmative government. But Congress was deemed more likely to embrace tax reduction than social spending, and Kennedy went along with the political logic.

His Harvard leave of absence expiring, Galbraith returned shortly before Kennedy went to Dallas. On 22 November 1963, Ken and I were lunching with the editors of *Newsweek* when the dreadful news came of the assassination. We flew back to Washington with Katharine Graham in anguish and despair. Thereafter, Lyndon Johnson, an old friend, offered him various jobs. In 1967 Johnson at Galbraith's behest intervened to save Andreas Papandreou, another Galbraith friend, from possible execution in Greece. But Galbraith's growing opposition to the Vietnam War soon cooled relations. The break with Johnson ended Galbraith's period of intimacy with Presidents.

By the mid-1960s, Galbraith was a national leader in the antiwar movement. In 1967, he took on the chairmanship of Americans for Democratic Action, acquiring a new platform from which to press the campaign against the war. The next year, he helped persuade Eugene McCarthy to run for the Democratic nomination as the antiwar candidate. When Robert Kennedy belatedly entered the race, Galbraith stuck by his original commitment. Still, he recognized that Kennedy would probably be the stronger candidate. In the first moments after Kennedy's victory in the California primary, he agreed that the time had come for liberals to unite behind Kennedy. After Kennedy's murder, Galbraith stayed with McCarthy to the turbulent end in Chicago, served as his foreign policy spokesman at the convention, and, in the autumn, determined to spare the nation the ignominy of Richard Nixon as President, campaigned energetically for Hubert Humphrey.

Four years later he worked hard for George McGovern, whom he considered, after John Kennedy's death, his "closest friend in politics, Edward Kennedy possibly excepted." In 1976 he backed Morris Udall for the Democratic nomination, in 1980 Edward Kennedy. "A commitment to losing causes," he wrote in 1981, "is still a constant in my life." As a loyal Democrat he voted for Jimmy Carter in both elections but had little contact with that curiously un-Democratic President. With Bill Clinton he has had affable personal relations, but the new political generation, like all new political generations, does not seek advice from octogenarians.

Galbraith has shown no inclination to abandon his long wrestle with the mythology of American politics. He retains the Keynesian faith in the power of ideas; "indeed, the world is ruled by little else." Power in his view is associated with knowledge; the major instrument for its exercise is persuasion. "The emancipation of belief is the most formidable of the tasks of reform and the one on which all else depends."

Nor has his enjoyment of politics slackened. He is a political economist to the last. Explaining the appeal of the political world, he has mentioned the charm of politics as theater, the pleasures it gives as a spectator (and as a participant) sport, its therapeutic value as an outlet for aggression; finally, "there is the thought that one is helping change the world."

That thought, he added, has its element of illusion. It does not appear that the world will be easily altered to Galbraithian specifications. But no one can doubt that his penetrating analysis, his joyous iconoclasm, his subversive wit, his serenity of perspective (he likes to quote Adam Smith after Burgoyne's surrender at Saratoga, "There's a lot of ruin in a nation"), and his generosity of spirit have contributed greatly to the future of liberal democracy as well as to the graces of human existence.

THE LUCKIEST JOURNEY
I EVER MADE

◆

Roy Jenkins

I HAVE KNOWN John Kenneth Galbraith for almost exactly half of his long life. He and his wife, Kitty Galbraith, first entertained me at dinner in 30 Francis Avenue (that unchanging background to their lives only a stone's long throw from Harvard Yard) on October 16, 1953. It was the day after his forty-fifth birthday, although I do not recollect any signs of a previous evening's bacchanalia being left either upon the house or upon the Galbraiths.

In the speech which I delivered at the Century Association in New York on the occasion of JKG's eightieth birthday, I described how that meeting came about and how much difference it has since made to my life. A month or so before, I had taken a plane from Detroit to New York. For the first hour it bumped a good deal, as was frequent in those pre-jet days. When the bumping ceased, my silent neighbors all suddenly became very loquacious. It turned out they were mostly economists, returning from some gathering of the American Economic Association. The chief among them, or at least the one I remember best, was Seymour Harris, I suppose the most devoted (but also distinguished) of Maynard Keynes's

American disciples. He invited me to Cambridge at the end of my American tour, which, it being the first time I had been in the United States, was long and comprehensive, and arranged for me to stay in the Dana-Palmer House, the elegant Harvard guest quarters on Quincy Street. When I got there, he performed a function which was for me still more important than his introduction of Keynes to the American public. He introduced me to Galbraith, and indeed to Arthur Schlesinger as well. This done, he then fell away, rather like the first stage booster in a rocket launch. I am not sure that I ever saw him again. But he had transformed my life, or at least its American dimension. Galbraith and Schlesinger responded with extraordinary generosity and hospitality to this foisting upon them of a young (thirty-two-year-old) and fairly obscure Labour MP. The Galbraith dinner party on Friday evening was followed by a Schlesinger one on Sunday. Between them they have ever since been to me an unfailing source of wit, friendship, vicarious repute, and hospitality. I count that 1953 Detroit flight the luckiest journey I ever made.

Amazing although it seems to me now, I did not revisit the United States for another six years. The Atlantic was still quite wide, both psychologically and in terms of time (circa eighteen hours by air or 4½ days by the great liners, which continued to take more than half of the 1950s traffic). But we remained in touch, although I have no record of our meeting again until September 1955, when we coincided at a Milan conference organized by the Congress for Cultural Freedom. It had a star-spangled intellectual cast, although the contribution I most vividly remember was that of a distinguished and not at all fellow-traveling (had he been that, he would hardly have been invited by that, as it subsequently emerged, CIA-financed organization) English professor of economics, who assured us that on existing trends the standard of living in the Soviet Union would overtake that of the United States in about ten years' time.

JKG at that stage was only a semifledged sage of the Western World. His appearance and delivery already gave him authority and aroused interest, but his books were then confined to *American Capitalism: The Concept of Countervailing Power* and *The Great Crash*, with *The Affluent Society* still three years in the future, and everything else still further off. He was still half thought of as an agricultural economist, which was how he had started, although clearly one who was not going to be confined by the bonds of acreage yields.

At the end of that conference Kitty drove me to Geneva, for which Ken had already departed, and I took her on to the roof of Milan Cathedral, with its great distant northern view of the arc of the Alps (Milanese smog was then less bad). She was overcome with vertigo, and I was seized with fear that I might be responsible for another Galbraith great crash. Disaster was, however, avoided, and I was at least thankful that it was Kitty's elfin form and not Ken's great height that I had to maneuver back to safety between the minarets and gargoyles.

That adventure fortunately seemed to solidify rather than rupture our quadripartite friendship. That autumn JKG dined with us in London (Kitty had returned to Massachusetts), and a few days after that I drove him down to Margate, on the easternmost tip of Kent, where that year's Labour Party Conference was taking place. As I at that time had a very small car, the eighty-mile journey must have been distinctly disagreeable for his long legs. I compensated by taking him to lunch with Hugh Gaitskell, the leader-in-waiting (he was elected two months later), which was the highest political honor I could then confer. Fortunately they got on very well. For the next three or four years relations proceeded happily on the basis of our having a Galbraith luncheon or dinner whenever one or both of them was in England. These were interspersed with increasingly vehement complaints that it was more than time that I come back to the United States, and that Jennifer visit it for the first time. I could counter only weakly by saying that in those days it was not all that easy for impoverished and relatively unknown MPs to get across the Atlantic, let alone take their wives with them. He, even before the success of *The Affluent Society* in 1958 made him a world figure, was, appropriately, much more affluent, certainly in terms of expenses-paid travel opportunities.

In 1959 he not only complained but did something constructive about it. He organized six or seven New England university lecture engagements, which between them made a month's visit for both of us perfectly viable. The visit was due to start on October 13, exactly five days after the British general election of that autumn. Looking back, I find that this must have implied a profound pessimism on my part about the likely outcome of that election. Had the Labour Party under Gaitskell won, I would certainly have been offered some sort of government job, although probably not of the rank of those which I was, paradoxically, to attain five years later, under the next leader, Harold Wilson, with whom my relations were much less friendly. And I could hardly have begun my first ministerial experience with four weeks in the United States.

My latent pessimism, although not generally shared at the beginning of the campaign, proved only too well founded, and Harold Macmillan was swept back in with an increased majority. This, however, did not free us for New England. It plunged the defeated Labour Party, as tends to be the way with parties in such circumstances, into deep crisis. What had gone wrong? Gaitskell and those close around him saw modernization and the abandonment of dogmatic baggage as the only route to future victory. This was a controversial course with the old Labourites of those days, sufficiently so to make me feel that I ought to be present and at Gaitskell's side for at least the first month of the new campaign.

I accordingly had to telephone JKG and tell him, at two days' notice, that I could not fulfill the engagements he had so generously set up. I remember vividly that I approached that call as, until then, one of the most forbidding of my life. What I cannot remember, at a distance of thirty-nine years, was whether it was I who had the temerity, or he the generosity, to suggest that I might still come in a month's time and do the rescheduled lectures in November rather than in October. That, at any rate, was the arrangement which emerged, with his having to undertake all the tedium and even embarrassment of having to negotiate all the readjustments. I have never doubted since that day that John Kenneth Galbraith, beyond his perhaps better-known attributes of wit, originality, and self-confidence, could be a man of exceptional kindness and, indeed, patience.

The visit, having survived these vicissitudes, could only have been either a great buttressing of friendship or the reverse. I am glad to say that it was the former. Several vignettes remain impressed on my mind: staying a total of nine nights in the interstices of Amherst, Dartmouth, Smith, Brandeis, etc., as well as excursions to New York and Washington, in the rambling Francis Avenue house; striding round Fresh Pond (JKG at least was striding; I was endeavoring to keep up) before lunch on Thanksgiving Day; another walk through the Business School on the far side of the Charles, with him expressing some fairly trenchant opinions about its intellectual inferiority to the real university on the other side of the river; our first glimpse (followed by many subsequent visits) of the recently acquired house above Newfane, Vermont, only for a winter picnic in front of a roaring fire, but with JKG embellishing the journey with a splendid account, as we passed his former house, of Harry Dexter White's relations with Keynes at Bretton Woods and of White's subsequent vicissitudes; and of JKG coming back from a New York meeting of the Democratic Advisory Council in a high state of exasperation with Dean Acheson, whose current Cold War rigidities were (at least temporarily) seen by JKG to be outweighing his outstanding service as Truman's Secretary of State. The whole experience was a wonderful education for me, not only in the pattern of East Coast universities and colleges, but also in American politics as seen from the liberal left of the Democratic Party. In these and other respects I was delighted to be an absorbent pupil.

Lest this essay be thought too hagiographic, I return to the last but one paragraph and relay some more irreverent thoughts and memories about JKG's self-confidence, as well as his wit and originality. At the eightieth birthday party, to which I have already referred, George Ball got a fine response to his claim that Ken's outstanding quality was, of course, his humility. I have witnessed several splendid examples of what I would prefer to call his supreme, unaffected, indestructible self-confidence. My favorite example comes from the late 1960s, when I was Chancellor of the Exchequer, and JKG, after dining with us alone in 11 Downing Street, suddenly and surprisingly expressed a desire to come with me to the House of Commons, where I had to perform the formal ten-minute act of voting in a division. I think he hoped to encounter and pay his respects (or vice-versa) to the Prime Minister, Harold Wilson. But as Wilson was not visible, he made do with greeting an ex-Prime Minister in the shape of Sir Alec Douglas Home. Home was as always impeccably courteous, but after about ten seconds it became apparent to me that, to his discredit, he did not really know who JKG was. After about another sixty seconds of desultory conversation, this became equally apparent to JKG. He was in no way disconcerted. As soon as we separated he turned to me and said, "Who was that man? I thought he was Alec Home." The logic was impeccable. If he did not know Galbraith, he could not be an ex-Prime Minister. The dismissal was complete.

Another, lesser example takes me back to 1960, the year of the Kennedy campaign and the year after my postponed 1959 visit. In mid-October we were again at the Galbraith house in the woods between Newfane and Townshend for the closing weekend of the season. On the Sunday morning JKG had taken us to see the beaver dams a short half mile from the house. Suddenly there was a great clanging of wires overhead. "That is my private home-made telephone alarm," he said, adding, "It will be the Senator" (and there was no doubt which senator he meant at that point in history). Whereupon he loped off through the undergrowth. When we got to the house we asked him what the Senator had wanted. "No," JKG said calmly, "it was the plumber from Brattleboro, but the Senator will be through soon." And so he was.

It was on that same Vermont visit that I took two friends to stay, and as we progressed with difficulty and after dark along the six miles of sometimes bewilderingly forking dirt road up from Newfane, one of them, well-schooled in *The Affluent Society*, said: "Well, we have certainly seen the public squalor on the way here. I only hope we see the private affluence when we arrive." So, up to a point, we did (and it was certainly fortified by the warmth of hospitality). But only up to a point. For while JKG would never think of not staying at the Carlyle Hotel in New York or the Ritz in London, neither he nor Kitty has ever believed in changing their domestic lifestyle to keep up with the royalties. The Francis Avenue house in Cambridge, Massachusetts, is fast qualifying as a house in a time warp. Happily, practically nothing changes. It ought eventually to become a national shrine, installed, probably by courtesy of Mrs. Charles Wrightsman, in a new extension to the Metropolitan Museum, and labeled New England Academic Interior, circa 1950. The remark on the way up the dirt road was also of course an objective tribute to JKG's outstanding ability to make phrases that resonate in the language and across the continents.

In the thirty-eight years that have gone by since that Kennedy-dominated October of hope and excitement, there have been many more notable (to me) Galbraith encounters. I never saw him in India, but I have read a lot about those 2 1/4 years of ambassadorship, which have left such a strong imprint on the lives of both Galbraiths. JKG is the most faithful sender of warmly inscribed copies of his books to his friends. As a result we have a complete collection, spanning the more than forty years from *American Capitalism* in 1952 to *Letters to Kennedy* in 1998. And they are not only a treasured possession (I wonder what such a complete autographed collection of Galbraithiana may be worth in, say, 2050), but have in addition all been read, with varying but never negligible degrees of profit. *Letters to Kennedy,* for instance, so far the last station on the line, may sound like scrapings from an old barrel, but it turned out to be a fascinating object lesson in how not to be put off by an unequal balance of power from delivering forthright, wise, elegant, and sometimes unwelcome advice. While I do not presume to achieve quite the wisdom or the eloquence, I intend to be much guided by them in my future dealings with Mr. Blair.

Our literary traffic has been two-way, but with me always

seeming to be the beneficiary. JKG has been immensely helpful to my publications in America. He wrote the foreword to the New York (1993) edition of my autobiography, *A Life at the Center,* and he has provided several most valuable prepublication puffs, most recently to my *Gladstone* (1997). There has also been a certain happy reciprocity about our trade in the somewhat inflated currency of honorary degrees. When I received the grand "court card" of a Harvard one in 1972 and was asked (mainly, it must be said, because Willy Brandt had canceled) to deliver the afternoon Commencement Address on the twenty-fifth anniversary of General Marshall's world-shaping speech on the same occasion, I did it all from the Galbraith house. I remember walking over with JKG, who cut well the most impressive figure in the Yard that morning. He towered above us all in a strawberry-colored gown and cap, which he said he got from some Scottish university (I forget which, and maybe he had too). It was embellished with two white strips of tape on each arm, then the symbol of support for the cause of equal numbers of women at Harvard. Eighteen years later I was able, early on in my chancellorship, to, as it were, return the compliment with an Oxford Honorary DCL, and to ensure that the Galbraiths did it from our house at East Hendred, just as I had gone to the steps of the Memorial Church in Harvard Yard from 30 Francis Avenue. This gave me great satisfaction, as I believe his presence and acceptance of the award did to the University of Oxford.

So I look back on my Galbraith friendship as one of the great enhancements of my life over nearly five decades. Above all it has given me pleasure, but also stimulus, intellectual satisfaction, and even a certain pride in being so generously embraced by such an unusual and indeed great figure of the second half of the twentieth century.

PERSONAL RECOLLECTIONS

◆

Katharine Graham

I FIRST CAME to know Ken Galbraith through my husband, Phil Graham. The friendship that developed between Phil and Ken in the early 1950s (and deepened later as they worked together on policy memos for then Senate Majority Leader Lyndon Johnson) was sealed in 1958, when Phil, who was a brilliantly selective reader, wrote a rave book review of *The Affluent Society* for the *Washington Post*.

Phil praised Ken for "sighting in the weaponry of his intelligence against what he terms 'the conventional wisdom' — that is, the fundamental ideas firmly held by most of us, firmly followed by leaders of almost all factions of all parties." Ken, who had labored over the book for the better part of five years, recalled how much Phil's review meant to him, especially in the face of a *Time* review describing it as a coffee-table book. (Ken tells me that *Time*'s comments were later repudiated by its then proprietor, Harry Luce.) Although Ken has written many books since *The Affluent Society*, probably none has had the extraordinary impact of this one.

Phil and Ken maintained a light-hearted correspondence over the years. Once, distressed at being referred to in the pages of the *Post* as "John K. Galbraith" instead of J.K.,

J. Kenneth, or Kenneth, with which designations he was "at home," Ken wrote Phil, revealing the reason for his aversion to "John." It seems that Ken was named for his Uncle John, who at one time was a rising figure in the Canadian farm implement business. However, by the time, as Ken put it, that "I was escaping teenage delinquency," Uncle John was "far gone in alcohol." Consequently, his strongly Calvinist family dropped the first name of John. Ken admitted that he never heard himself referred to as John "without discomfort and some wonder if I might be running a slight risk with the next cocktail."

Always one with a way with words, Ken, together with Arthur Schlesinger and John Bartlow Martin, went through two campaigns as a speech writer for Adlai Stevenson. Thinking Adlai was not going to run in 1960, both Ken and Arthur became early participants in John F. Kennedy's campaign. Throughout that campaign, and continuing for the three years of his presidency, Ken added to Kennedy's thinking, certainly on economic subjects but on others as well.

From the beginning of the Kennedy Administration, Ken's voice was heard. He was sent by the President-elect to his old Senate office to put a final polish on Ted Sorensen's memorable inaugural speech. One sentence in the speech struck him as being rather abrupt, so he inserted the words "Let us begin . . ." Also, he felt there was a little too much Cold War quality to the speech, so he suggested the unforgettable sentence "Let us never negotiate out of fear, but let us never fear to negotiate."

Ken became an integral part of the Kennedy brain trust and was always ready with advice for the President. Once Ken left for India, where the President had sent him as ambassador, along with Kitty, to represent our country, much of the advice came in letters, which we now have the benefit of seeing in print. Ken's voluminous correspondence to the President was interspersed with visits home to try to ensure that his ideas were being implemented.

These trips home caused great concern among the more conservative administration economists, who disagreed with many of Ken's views—Ken was, of course, against cutting taxes and for more spending on social programs. They found this situation understandably problematic and asked the State Department to warn them when Ken was coming, which came to be called the "Galbraith early warning system."

All of his life, Ken has been a very concentrated, indefatigable worker. No matter what he was "officially" doing—teaching at Harvard, politicking, or being ambassador—Ken was always writing. His books, articles, reviews, and letters to friends (and to editors) are innumerable. While it seems that his writing comes effortlessly, Ken assures me that he long ago learned the importance of revision and then further revision. He once confessed to me that "I never put the note of spontaneity that my critics like so much in anything prior to the fifth draft. Then I make it spontaneous."

Also in the category of confessions having to do with his writing, Ken told me that once he has written a first draft in longhand, his longtime assistant, Andrea Williams, puts that draft on the computer, correcting his spelling and pointing out repetition here or there. He admitted that she has the most infuriating habit of putting the comment "not clear" on almost every page and seems to have been resistant over the years to his attempts to persuade her that "my academic reputation depends occasionally on obfuscation." Ken has concluded that "writers who think that they are subject to some Shakespearean inspiration that makes their first drafts somehow priceless, they're absolutely wrong."

When Ken is not writing, he is most certainly reading. In

March of 1961, when I was subjected to forced bed rest because of a mild case of tuberculosis, Ken came to see me. He had been particularly eager to visit, since he himself had had tuberculosis when he was about twenty and knew the restrictions it imposed. This required recuperative period was for me a time of mixed feelings, an ambiguous experience. As Ken and I sat on the back terrace of my house, he told me how much he had loved his own forced total idleness, because it allowed him to read uninterruptedly.

Ken's mind is awhirl even when he is supposedly at leisure. Whether skiing on his winter vacations in Switzerland or walking and entertaining at his Vermont farm, he enjoys life to the fullest.

Ken's fighting liberal views have not diminished with advancing years. He believes strongly in the privileges of publishers—and the responsibilities. We had an exchange of letters in late 1969 in which he lectured me:

> And I do think you are being far too discreet. You are supposed to be the head of a great publishing enterprise which holds vigorous, liberal opinions. There is nothing wrong with that. As Mr. Dulles so well said, "Neutrality is immoral." And if it isn't immoral, it is certainly not very interesting . . .
>
> P.S. I was always brought up to believe that the crusading publishers were the best. Is that wrong?

I must have written back piously about news-reporting having to be straight and detached, because Ken wrote back two weeks later, protesting:

> I am not necessarily for partisanship; by crusading, I had no such thing in mind. But I am persuaded that a newspa-

per must be a vehicle for convictions. I hope these are ones with which I agree; but the worst of all papers is one without a point of view . . . For purely technical reasons, it can't be exclusively your point of view; too many other people are involved. And I subscribe broadly to the need to separate fact from opinion. But having said all that, it seems to me that your opinions must show and must show clearly, and if yours do not emerge, whose will? If you are going to be a purely neutral administrator, you should turn the whole thing over to somebody from the Harvard Business School.

Another exchange ensued the following year. Government people, Ken thought, should not call up and complain to those of us in the press. Ken believed that the differences were often matters of political point of view. I believe, however, that this kind of communication can be an important steam valve. People from every sector, including the government, need to be able to voice their concerns or disagreements and know that they are heard.

Ken and I continue our correspondence and our conversations, as we have for forty years, seeming to pick right up where we last left off. His is a New Deal voice that grew stronger over the years, in its clarity and force, in its humor and irony. This smart and hard-working, values-laden man was a Canadian farm boy who grew up to put himself on the front lines of the Keynesian revolution. As he said in his memoirs: "My legacy was the inherent insecurity of the farm-reared boy in combination with an aggressive feeling that I owed it to all I encountered to make them better informed." With his classic study *The Great Crash: 1929,* and *The Scotch,* and *A Journey Through Economic Time*—and with every other book he has written—Ken, indeed, has informed us all, defining so much (from the affluent society to the new industrial state) and contributing to our own conventional wisdom.

Ken Galbraith is many things to many people: economist, lecturer, teacher, editor, author, visionary, "abiding liberal." Beyond these, to so many of us he is a great and constant friend.

GALBRAITH AS A
CITIZEN OF THE UNIVERSITY

———◆———

Derek Bok

GALBRAITH," said a senior colleague over lunch years ago at the Faculty Club, "is like the paprika in a stew. Without it, the dish would make pretty dull eating."

Presumably, my companion meant that Galbraith played a unique role as a member of the Harvard faculty, imparting a special flavor to the university that gave it a distinctive personality and helped to make it more vivid and memorable. But what did that flavor consist of, and how was it achieved? Only gradually over the years has the answer taken shape in my mind, and even now my understanding is undoubtedly far from complete.

Prior to World War II, as a young economist, Galbraith came to know my parents-in-law, Gunnar and Alva Myrdal, during a visit to Stockholm. Because of this acquaintance, my wife and I were invited to meet Ken and Kitty very soon after we had arrived at Harvard, in 1958, where I was to begin my duties as an assistant professor in the Law School. In the years that followed, there were many more visits to the Galbraiths' home—some for meals with one or both of my parents-in-law; some in the company of other children of friends, most of them undergraduates, who came for an evening of conversation, often with one of the well-known politicians and public figures who trooped regularly in and out of the house at 30 Francis Avenue.

These occasions gave me an impression of Galbraith as a public intellectual and a family friend. They revealed his interest in young people, his loyalty and kindness to friends, his love of lively conversation about public affairs. But in the Harvard of those days, a vast distance separated the world of Galbraith's Economics Department and that of the Law School faculty. As a result, it was only after fate had propelled me into a twenty-year effort to preside over Harvard's fluctuating fortunes that I came to know him as a faculty member and a citizen of the university.

I soon realized that Galbraith took a keen interest in Harvard affairs and had a deep concern for the welfare of the university. He did not express this interest in the usual ways, by volunteering for committees or for the chairmanship of his department. Indeed, he tended to escape these mundane assignments simply by virtue of being too iconoclastic, independent, and unpredictable to be sought after for such posts. Yet his was a strong institutional loyalty that deserves some explanation, since it was something he rarely talked about, let alone advertised. Indeed, in some respects it is at odds with his public reputation.

To the outside world, Galbraith must have seemed the quintessential jet-setting professor—often appearing on television or in the pages of the newspaper, forever flying to the four corners of the earth to attend conferences, traveling to Washington to consult, and taking two years off for an ambassadorship to India. But Galbraith had another side, as well. He belonged to an earlier generation of professors who believed that outside activities should be balanced by services rendered to one's university that went beyond simply meeting one's classes and writing books.

Galbraith's particular form of service was definitely unusual, sometimes taking the form of open dissent from the policies of those who presided over Harvard and sought to administer its affairs. Perhaps the well-known opposition to his appointment by several members of the Board of Overseers made him forever dubious about the wisdom of those august gentlemen (later ladies, too) who sat on Harvard's governing boards. Perhaps he was simply born with a playful irreverence toward authority. Whatever the cause, Galbraith was noted for taking public issue with a number of university policies and practices—the choice of candidates for honorary degrees, the anonymity of Harvard's governing boards and their lack of familiarity with academic life, the shift in the Economics Department toward more and more technical, quantitative research, the administration's response to student protests in the late 1960s.

Not all of Galbraith's causes were pursued in public. For example, he once asked to see me because he was worried about Harvard's investment policies. Some readers may be surprised to learn that he did not wish to discuss the propriety of investing in companies doing business in South Africa, nor did he protest our holding stock in tobacco companies (since discontinued). Instead, he arrived with a list of complaints ranging from the tendency of Harvard managers to invest in too many stocks (impossible to keep adequate track of so many companies) to their proclivity for making venture capital investments that Galbraith considered too risky. All of his concerns were thoughtfully considered, all were carefully reviewed, and most turned out to have merit. The point, however, is not to praise Galbraith's investment acumen but rather to call attention to his willingness to take the time and trouble to examine a subject of no small importance to Harvard, even though he had no personal stake in the outcome.

Others acts of support were equally private but no less

indicative of his underlying loyalty to the institution. Soon after I had taken office, he wrote me a letter—the only such letter I ever received—predicting that economic conditions would be difficult for universities over the next few years and requesting, as a result, that he receive no further increases in salary. Not many years later, I received another letter, this one asking to retire well before the maximum age of seventy on the ground that he had always believed in giving opportunities to the young and that now was the time to put his principles into practice. Better known than these examples are the gifts he has given to Harvard over the years, ranging from the royalties from his book *The Affluent Society* to the teaching prize he established in the Economics Department, the room he helped raise money for to honor his friends Merle and Johnny Fainsod, and the transfer to the Fogg Museum of his exquisite collection of Indian miniature paintings.

It is also important not to overlook his role in helping to enliven Harvard and Cambridge as a social and intellectual community. Galbraith has never been one of those distant figures who are too busy to partake of the university's social life and boast of having more friends on Capitol Hill than in their own immediate neighborhood. No observant person could come to the Galbraiths' for a birthday gathering or an anniversary celebration without noticing how many people were there who lived within a few blocks of 30 Francis Avenue. In addition, Galbraith has long been a familiar figure at the table in the Faculty Club reserved for members from all parts of the university who have no business to transact but merely wish to eat and exchange ideas. For as long as I can remember, he has been prominently in attendance at all manner of university events, from public lectures to the annual Christmas carol service at Memorial Church. I have never known him to miss a Harvard Commencement, and it would be hard not to keep track, since he towers above the crowd of faculty colleagues and is always flamboyantly attired in an exotic robe from one of the far-flung universities that have honored him with degrees. During graduation day, the garden party that he and Kitty have given for so many years has become almost as much a part of the annual rites as the morning exercises in the Yard.

What, then, is the larger significance of Galbraith's role within the university? In an important sense, my faculty colleague was correct. More than any other living faculty member, Galbraith *is* the paprika in Harvard's stew. Without him, the university would lose much of its distinctive flavor. More than any single person in the past several decades, he has given Harvard a reputation as a university engaged with the problems of society, a place of social criticism, intellectual controversy, and high excitement.

But Galbraith's part in defining Harvard's external reputation cannot do justice to his significance to the university, because it neglects his role *within* the institution. Much has been written about the contemporary university as a place where itinerant professors live and draw a paycheck for a time before moving on to some other palace of learning that will pay them more, build them bigger laboratories, and promise to appoint more colleagues with similar interests. For such professors, loyalties seem to run primarily to themselves, secondarily to their disciplines, with universities finishing a distant third. Of course, universities are not unique in this respect. Something similar has happened to baseball teams, corporations, law firms, and many other organizations. Institutional loyalty no longer seems to be in style.

It is worth remembering that things have not always been this way. The strongest postwar universities have benefited from a cadre of professors who spent the bulk of their academic careers in one place, gaining unusual distinction in their professions but also manifesting great loyalty to their institution and taking real pleasure in helping to build it and defend it.

In his unique way, Galbraith has been a part of this tradition, if not as a team player (which he has never pretended to be), then certainly as a faculty member prepared to invest considerable time and energy beyond the requirements of his office to make Harvard a better place. His efforts were not always appreciated by the university administration or even by his colleagues. But the passage of time affords a better perspective than these transient reactions with which to judge his contributions.

Looking back over fifty years of Galbraith's continuous association with the Harvard faculty, one must surely count him as one of Harvard's leading citizens who has added to its reputation, enlivened its conversations, enhanced its social life, and fought to keep the institution on a humane and honorable path. Many of his proposals to improve the university have been adopted in the fullness of time, often without acknowledgment but always to the benefit of the institution. Perhaps Harvard could not accommodate an unlimited number of colleagues with such an irreverent wit and a critical eye. But Harvard—like all universities—can never have enough professors who believe that helping to build and preserve the quality of their institution is both a satisfying pursuit in its own right and an important part of their responsibilities as members of a faculty.

On Class Day in 1975, when the senior class honored Galbraith by choosing him to be their speaker, he remarked:

> Harvard has always had two kinds of professors, the inside people and the outside people. The insiders make their lives within the university community; the outsiders are

only associated with it. The outside men — most of us, alas, have been men — are the best known; the insiders are the most useful.

There is much truth to this statement. Yet in the end, the most useful professors of all have been those special few who somehow manage to bridge both worlds, making important contributions to the outside world *and* to the life of the university. In his unique way, Galbraith must be counted among this small but essential group.

BIG MAN,
LITTLE PICTURES

───────◆───────

Stuart Cary Welch

W<small>HEN A MAN</small> of John Kenneth Galbraith's scale, accomplishment, charisma, and breadth of interest discovered Indian painting, something was bound to happen. It did, to the benefit of a delectable but once neglected field of art, and to Harvard University. While he was ambassador to India, from 1961 to 1963, circumstances encouraged him to further a longstanding interest in Indian miniature painting. He became captivated by Rajput paintings shown to him by Mohinder Singh Randhawa, a kindred spirit and a fellow "Renaissance man." An officer in the Indian Civil Service, Randhawa was an ardent lover of paintings from the Punjab Hills and author of many books and articles about them. He extolled their merits so compellingly that Ambassador Galbraith soon joined the ranks of enthusiasts. Another influence in Ken's devotion to Indian miniatures was W. G. (Bill) Archer, also an Indian Civil Service Officer, who later was the keeper of Indian art in the Victoria and Albert Museum. He was the author of the monumental *Indian Paintings from the Punjab Hills.*

Galbraith, Randhawa, and Archer shared many enthusiasms, starting as enlightened amateurs rather than full-time life-long art "professionals." They belonged to a generation that had been taught to admire Pre-Raphaelite painting, so their eyes were prepared for exquisitely painted Hill miniatures inhabited by manly heroes reminiscent of Sir Gawain and by graceful heroines strikingly akin to Dante Gabriel Rossetti's classically "English" belles. Hill pictures provided seductive antidotes to painful memories and to the tribulation of current administrative chores. Although this trio of activists might not have admitted it, they warmed to pictures usually described as "beautiful" and "romantic."

When Canadian-born Ken was shown Kangra pictures, a keen mind and idealistic spirit nurtured within the British Empire had found an art to which he was perfectly attuned. Like India-loving Archer and scientist–art historian Randhawa, Ken was vulnerable not to the avant-garde abstractions perkily described by Harry Truman as "ham and egg art" (Jackson Pollock et al.) but to gentle, slightly nostalgic, dependably ingratiating miniature paintings.

Ken became an eager collector of them at a time when they were profusely available. Moreover, Ken—who shares everything, including a marvelous range of people—enjoyed showing his discoveries to friends. Small pictures do well at small gatherings. Unlike murals, panel pictures, or framed canvases, they encourage amicable cheek-by-jowl closeness. Created for enjoyment at court, these small delights are seen to best advantage among friends and family.

Because these lively opaque watercolors are vulnerable to light, damp, and insects, they were securely wrapped in bandanas and kept in *pothikhanas* (picture storage), whence they were brought out for occasional inspection. In circumstances that would have pleased the original patrons and artists there were scenes of Galbraithian hospitality at the American embassy in New Delhi, where the guests included Jawaharlal

Nehru, Mme. Pandit, assorted former—but still distinguished —maharajahs, and John and Jacqueline Kennedy.

One of the many attractive qualities of these compact pictures from the Hills is their elegance, a characteristic that it is not difficult to extend to their owners and admirers. If from their paintings we sense this quality, we can also sense it in Ken and Kitty Galbraith, who have not only appreciated the nuances of color, line, form, and depth of feeling or characterization seen in the pictures, but whose lives have been imbued with the beauty of their pictures. At the risk of embarrassing Ken, it should be observed that if one admires his intelligence, social responsibility, aplomb, wit, and selfless generosity, one also admires his personal elegance.

After Ken's return from India in 1963, he resumed his position as professor of economics at Harvard University. But neither India nor Indian painting was forgotten. He enthusiastically and effectively masterminded "Gods, Thrones, and Peacocks," one of the earlier exhibitions of Indian pictures held in the United States. I first became aware of Ken's exciting plan when he invited me to see his pictures, which enlivened the walls of the Galbraith house on Francis Avenue. Following him from one room to the next, I hugely enjoyed the collection. Never before had I seen paintings so "personally" displayed. Literally, they were over my head, hung not at the usual museum sight line, but at the Galbraith elevated level. Sympathizing with the plight of midgets, I climbed on chairs for a close look, and what I saw brought delight.

While remaining extremely modest about the merit of his own pictures (he insists that his collection includes only a few "masterpieces"), Ken spread the word about Indian painting. His pictures thrilled and enlightened Jacqueline Kennedy, adding exoticism to eyes already widely opened to most other kinds of world art; and through her, Ken's contagious pleasure progressed into the White House. International eminences — Christians of every persuasion, Jews, Muslims, agnostics, and more than a few nature worshipers — learned to appreciate Rajput painting. Ultimately thanks to Ken, Lord Krishna, the Indian "Apollo," and his beloved Radha found new devotees.

Although Ken's taste was keen and sure, he enjoyed discussing his paintings with so-called specialists. Looking at his pictures with him was stimulating and fun. Not only was I honored to be shown a splendid collection, but I was flattered at being so well received by one of America's—indeed, the world's—major economists and wits. This experience enriched my understanding of Indian art and taught me about Ken and about his sagacious wife, Kitty. Both were kind, generous, and lively. If only Zoffany, the eighteenth-century German-born English painter of Indian "conversation pieces," had been available to record the *Domestic Scenes with Pictures* we enjoyed! I recall with pleasure the evening when Ken brought to my house a magnificent seventeenth-century Basholi picture from a well-known Rasamanjari series, surely his boldest and most strikingly colorful picture. While discussing this stunning portrayal of a *nayika* (heroine) and her lover (resembling Lord Krishna himself), the ex-ambassador sat on the floor. At the time, this consideration for the discrepancy in our respective statures went unnoticed, so intense was his concentration. Later, I understood it as yet another instance of Ken's natural, unselfconscious grace, one of the qualities that has brought him so many friends among students, colleagues, and the general public.

Because Ken so enjoyed sharing his works of art, "Gods, Thrones, and Peacocks" was held in four institutions, the Asia House Gallery in New York City, the Baltimore Museum of

Art, Munson-Williams-Proctor Institute of Utica, New York, and the Fogg Museum of Art at Harvard. Empowered by Ken's enthusiasm, the catalogue was written by the present author, assisted by his then student Milo Cleveland Beach. To quote from the introduction, the exhibition was "intended to bring out the variety, power and charm of later northwestern Indian miniature painting, as shown in a selection of pictures from several collections, and to trace . . . the relationship between two main streams of tradition, one indigenous, the other foreign." Most of the pictures were lent by Ken, with additions from Jacqueline Kennedy, the Fogg Museum, and the present author. Launched by the reputations of Mrs. Kennedy and former Ambassador Galbraith, the show was extremely well attended at all venues and received critical acclaim. At the Harvard opening, Jacqueline Kennedy was escorted from picture to picture by Ken, and for a second look by the curator.

Invariably generous, Ken often provides glorious surprises; perhaps supreme among them was his gift to Harvard of virtually all of his excellent Indian paintings, a major addition to the university's collection of Indian art. Although such previous donors as Grenville Winthrop, Edward W. Forbes, Abby Aldrich Rockefeller, Paul J. Sachs, and John Goelet had provided Harvard students with firsthand access to remarkable Arab, Persian, Turkish, and Mughal paintings and drawings, the university's collections of Rajput pictures were meager. Thanks to Ken Galbraith, an essential link was added to the chain of art. Harvard could boast a splendid and harmoniously balanced collection representing in depth the entire span of Turko-Indo-Iranian painting.

In 1968, Houghton Mifflin published Mohinder Singh Randhawa's and John Kenneth Galbraith's *Indian Painting: The Scene, Themes, and Legends,* a substantial and lucidly written introduction to the subject. It is suggested on the dust jacket of the book that Ken accepted the post of ambassador to India in order to further his interest in Indian painting—which is probably more an example of Galbraithian irony than a publisher's blurb. This splendidly illustrated book was inspired, in the early spring of 1963, when Ken and M.S. visited the Kangra Valley. In the foreword they wrote, "We decided to write a book about this valley and its rulers, courts, and people and their painters. Presently we expanded the enterprise to tell of the other rulers, courts, great and small, where painting flourished." Devotees of Indian painting are grateful.

Ken's love for Indian pictures continues. His extraordinary gift of his own fine collection to Harvard was a painful sacrifice, hence all the more poignant to those who gain from it. He and Kitty often come to see the pictures that were once (and, we like to believe, continue to be) theirs; and when Harvard's curators bring them out for major exhibitions—just as these vulnerable masterpieces once emerged from *pothikhanas*—there among the students and other visitors, savoring the delight, are the Galbraiths.

ON GALBRAITH'S

ECONOMIC, SOCIAL,

AND POLITICAL

IDEAS

◆

THE PENDULUM
SWINGS BACK

———————◆———————

Will Hutton

I<small>T IS GOOD</small> that John Kenneth Galbraith has lived to see these times. The pendulum, which had swung so far away from the values and economic philosophy in which he believes, has begun to swing back. It is not just that there is a financial panic in Asia extending to Wall Street, inducing conditions analogous to those of the Crash of 1929 and reminding us of his famous book; it is that everywhere there is a stepping back from the extreme claims made by the neo-conservatives. He is about to reap the reward of a long life in which he has stayed true to the principles and insights of his youth. If economists could ever sink their differences and raise an unqualified hooray, it should be for him.

However, intellectual fashion is not quite like skirt lengths. The pendulum may swing, but not to the same place it occupied before. If there are renewed doubts about the endless felicity of markets and extension of private enterprise into every walk of economic and social life, that does not mean there is a renewed interest in socialism or even social democracy. On the contrary. The search is on for a so-called third way, which avoids the pitfalls of socialist planning, overstrong trade unions, and widespread public ownership while seeking to avert the worst inequities of unbridled capitalism. The search need not go very far. Galbraith has been preaching the merits of this position and developing what it might mean for all his adult life; if there is an intellectual father of these sets of ideas, it is he.

So far, the "third-wayers" have not dared embrace the full-blooded Galbraithian vision; after all, he is a liberal Keynesian who believes that governments have a duty to alleviate inequality, sponsor public enterprise where the market must fail, and regulate aggressively, even plan, in the public interest. He sees growth originating not in some mysterious spirit of entrepreneurship spreading its grace as long as markets operate freely, but in almost the opposite fashion; it is through the interaction of the big battalions—large firms and their capacity to innovate—and government, sponsoring research and investing in human and physical capital—that the wellsprings of economic growth are grounded. In macroeconomic policy Galbraith is a Keynesian; in micropolicy an advocate of endogenous-growth theory long before the term was invented; in social policy an unashamed believer in redistribution and public action.

This is an altogether too interventionist brew for the Clinton and Blair governments, who want to define the third way in more modest terms. They see little chance of modifying or regulating contemporary capitalism in any major way, even if they could construct a robust enough intellectual and political coalition to do the job—which they doubt and, in any case, are unconvinced they want to do. Instead, they are adopting a more cautious and limited agenda, still cast within the intellectual framework of the right. In fiscal and monetary policy they are conservatives, preferring to explain unemployment as a "supply-side" failure rather than as something intrinsic to the operation of capitalism. In their social policy, they remain punitive and ungenerous, attempting to promote social cohesion and inclusion through " tough" microinterventions—naming and shaming, robust policing, zero tolerance of crime, making welfare conditional on willingness to work, and the like. However, there are areas in which they are tiptoeing toward a Galbraithian position, defending the provision of "public" goods like education, science, transport, and health by the state with more confidence, and in Britain launching an ambitious welfare-to-work program. As the right weakens in both countries, there are signs that the Blair and Clinton governments could yet gain more confidence.

Galbraith, like all of us occupying the same broad intellectual position, is in something of a quandary over how to approach the new third way. He is supportive where it chimes in with his own preconceptions, but chafes over its caution and conservatism. In general, though, he is skeptical about the efficacy of this policy mix and, in particular, about its intellectual credentials. The Blairite kind of third way is distinct from the conservatism that preceded it, certainly, but it is part of the same family of ideas. There is a basic trust in the operation of capitalism and an unwillingness to challenge the income inequalities it throws up. The paradigm remains "trickle-down" economics, in which the poor essentially take their chance; the underlying assumption is that they are shirkers and welfare cheats, needing to be cajoled into working by threats of loss of income if they stay on benefits too long.

Nobody has mocked this position with more deadly barbs than Galbraith. Only those with no experience of life at the bottom could imagine for a moment that the real privation and, more important, loss of sense of self-worth, by being so far below even average lifestyles, are circumstances in which the disadvantaged choose to be. One of Kenneth Galbraith's great appeals is his humanity, and he would not need to be told the latest research that links male suicide not to absolute but to relative poverty. Individuals benchmark themselves by others in their society in the here and now, and if they see that even modest lifestyles and opportunities are out of their reach, they cannot help devaluing their own worth to the point that for some suicide seems justifiable. Your life seems of so little value that it is expendable. The rise in young male suicides in Britain in a deregulated labor market—with falling real wages for young people, along with job insecurity—has produced results that Galbraith would consider wholly predictable.

He has always contested the argument that a strong welfare state, moderate levels of taxation, job security, and effective trade unions are the enemies of growth and employment. He has been sometimes a lone voice, disregarded as an eccentric by his peers, in viewing the welfare state as an indispensable instrument for pooling risk and offering minimal levels of security, especially for those at the bottom. It is a means of expressing social solidarity while redistributing income. All get something by way of health care, pensions, and unemployment relief, but all pay something. It is both social glue and an active means of alleviating insecurity, risk, and poverty.

Galbraith repudiates the counterargument—that welfare is somehow unaffordable—with a mixture of good jokes and acute observations about human nature. The constituency of contentment, the 40 percent in secure full-time jobs and middle-class lifestyles who can afford to provide for themselves, are certainly against welfare, deploying the eternal arguments that have been used against poor relief. Help will degrade the moral character of the poor and their incentive to find work.

But the problem of the poor is not solved by making them poorer and more at risk to the vagaries of the labor market. It may be true that government expenditure can be lowered by privatizing the welfare system, but the risks faced by the poor do not disappear. They may now be off the public sector's balance sheet, but they have not disappeared. The supposition that they will now be "incentivized" to get work that they formerly shirked is, for Galbraith, an intolerable slur on human nature; of course they were looking for work beforehand and would like to be in different circumstances. All that has been achieved is that the problem has been swept under the carpet and people who did not deserve the fate have become paupers.

I recall once proposing that we write a joint article, setting out the case for progressive taxation. He replied that he would agree only if I accepted that any just system of taxation had to be calibrated by the protests of the rich: the more just, the more they would complain. It was only when their protests became really shrill that you could know you had pitched your tax rates high enough. The idea that low taxes were in some respect a key incentive to work has always struck him as being the self-serving argument of the rich; people will try to make as much money as they can whatever the tax rate, and avoid it however high or low. He would rather turn the argument on its head: taxation is the downpayment every citizen makes to live in a just society with a satisfactory supply of public goods, redistribution of income to the poor, and an infrastructure of welfare support. It is only if society has such a moral order at its core that it can be midwife to successful capitalism, and so avoid the descent into the license, spivvery, and cronyism to which every capitalist system is prone. We never got to write the article; maybe we will soon.

Of course capitalists themselves can be relied upon never to see the danger, and to argue with every breath in their bodies that taxes should be low, government spending minimal, regulation nonexistent, welfare outlays based on targeted and means-tested relief for the very poor, and no constraint whatsoever laid upon the so-called wealth-creating private sector. It is this self-serving credo that has been given dignity by classical economics, whose axioms, while purporting to have the status of universal truths, are based upon the partisan interests of the very well-off. The notions that we are rational pursuers of self-interest, that power and information are or can be equally distributed, and that markets correspond to some force of nature are propaganda for the advantaged, so that they can pretend the system that most particularly benefits them benefits all. Galbraith started saying this fifty years ago, and he says it still; he has been a standard bearer all his life, not merely for a Keynesian view of how the market system operates, but for a humorous restatement of a simple, liberal moral position. The proposition is stark: we look after everyone in order to look after ourselves, for unless we do, capitalism's intrinsic barbarities will sooner or later create popular rebellion and so undermine the very system on whose vitality we all depend.

This is true not just at home but abroad. Galbraith is the quintessential internationalist, seeing clearly how the success of national economic and social arrangements are intertwined with the structure of the international economy. It was never likely that an intellectual who argued the case for regulation and planning at home would suspend the argument abroad. Nor has he. He has watched the development of global financial markets along with ever more ingenious devices for speculation—so-called financial derivatives—

with alarm, especially as the economic ideology of the markets is unashamedly conservative.

His unexpected ally in a critique that remains a preoccupation of only a minority is George Soros. It is rather a curious spectacle, the ninety-year-old doyen of liberal Keynesianism, making common cause with the dark prince of financial speculation; but their target is the same. Markets panic, driving financial valuations to absurd lows at an incredible pace and demanding a speed of adjustment of the real economy, which is beyond the capacity of any to deliver—and which, in any case, involves unnecessary unemployment, loss of investment, and public-spending cuts. The solution to this phenomenon is not to carry the "marketization" and exposure of national economies to global financial markets yet further, as the international orthodoxy insists, but to change the rules of engagement. Financial markets should have less destabilizing power, not more.

Events in Asia over the last twelve months have amply demonstrated the power of Galbraith's thesis. Japan, the heart of the Asian economy, is mired in a recession whose fundamental cause is a deficiency of demand. It is amplified by a banking system plagued by bad debts incurred by earlier misguided overenthusiasms. The smaller economies of Asia, ranging from Korea's to Indonesia's, are victims of a witless wave of indiscriminate speculation, forcing colossal and destabilizing economic contractions, whatever the national circumstances, and which has spread like a contagion to Russia and, most recently, Latin America. The danger, only belatedly recognized in Washington, London, Paris, and Bonn, is that as the financial crisis extends throughout the West it will prompt a world credit crunch and, in consequence, a world recession.

The debate about the appropriate policy response is a curious amalgam of the new conservative orthodoxy, together with a reluctant recognition of old Keynesian verities. Every Western economist calls upon the Japanese to reflate through higher government spending, since successive tax cuts have failed, and to unconditionally underwrite the banking system. But such Keynesian remedies are neglected or ignored when it comes to the international financial system. Here, the "Washington consensus" continues to argue for free capital flows, open borders, floating exchange rates, the priority of keeping inflation low, and minimal regulation. If the financial markets are not working perfectly, that is because there is insufficient "transparency" and poor "information," rather than because they have an intrinsic capacity to move between excessive fear and optimism.

So while a Galbraithian analysis is cheerfully adopted for the ills of Japan, it is largely suspended when the rest of Asia is debated. The sharp recessions in almost every Asian country are regarded as the proper punishment for their adopting a variant of crony capitalism and rigging their financial markets, notably by pegging their exchange rates to the appreciating dollar and not deregulating their banking systems rapidly enough. It does not matter that government spending and borrowing have typically been low, that inflation is well under control, and investment and savings high; these countries deserve their fate. They must open up more to the international capital markets and organize their economies around the American model.

This is not merely breathtakingly arrogant and intellectually inconsistent; it is a poor way of explaining what went wrong in Asia and why. It was only two or three years ago that these same economies were being lauded for their very high growth rates and distinctive approach to economic development. Their emphasis on stable ownership, investment in human capital, linkages between the financial and industrial sectors, export orientation, and high domestic savings—together with some form of indicative planning—were correctly seen as offering a new route to rapid economic growth.

Now their proponents are written off as crony capitalists exposed for falsely rigging markets, but the truth is that they are in part victims of their own success and in part victims of an irrational panic of the financial markets that is inherent to their operation. Every Asian country had, by the mid-1990s, pegged its exchange rate to the dollar, both to demonstrate to international investors that it had an effective counterinflation strategy and to assure them that they would run no exchange risk if they invested in the country concerned. It was a double whammy that allowed extra marginal inward investment and an assurance of low inflation, and, as long as the dollar depreciated against the yen, a key competitive advantage against the Japanese.

As a policy, however, it broke down under two key influences. The IMF, OECD, and Western finance ministries were not satisfied with dollar-pegs alone; they wanted to open up the financial markets of the fastest-growing area of the world economy to their own banks and financial institutions, which meant that the tight system of regulation, licensing, capital controls, and credit direction that each Asian economy had developed had to be dismantled to allow foreigners to participate. Throughout the late 1980s and early 1990s, the Asian economies duly obliged, producing results similar to the financial deregulation of the U.S. and U.K. economies in the 1980s; there was a credit boom.

This again is not difficult to explain if you inhabit a Galbraithian universe. The first consequence of financial deregulation is that banks will be freer to lend than they were before, and for an individual bank, there is no reason not to lend even if the lending proposition does not conform to what used to be considered good banking criteria. If it does not lend, someone else will. The act of that lending itself, along with a myriad of similar lending decisions, generates such credit growth and inflation of asset values that the decision becomes validated—and so the process goes on, until asset values get so inflated and personal, and corporate balance sheets so distended, that the process breaks down.

Such a process took place across Asia in the early and mid 1990s, lifting already high growth rates to stratospheric levels, but generating strong domestic inflationary pressures whose impact was capped temporarily by the pegged exchange rates. What triggered crisis conditions, however, was the collapse of the yen and the associated rise in the dollar, along with the powerful entry of China into the world trading system. Thai, Korean, Indonesian, Malaysian, and Philippine exports fell away sharply under the twin impact of currency appreciation and Chinese competition, and all countries began to run unsustainable current account deficits. The pegged exchange rates became obvious one-way bets for the hedge funds, and Soros led a speculative attack with only one possible result: the regional collapse of the pegged exchange rate system.

But the falls in the currencies were not the 5, 10, or 15 percent needed to make rational adjustments to the flow of exports and imports; they fell by this degree in a day. The weight of financial market speculation now possible with financial derivatives, together with the capacity for mobile capital to exit a country with no let or hindrance, produced astonishing percentage falls in currencies and bond and share prices. What is worse, they set in train a real economic contraction that was and is completely unjustified by the underlying economic fundamentals. Falls in GDP now promise to exceed 10 percent in some countries, notwithstanding high savings ratios, small public sectors, and very prudent fiscal policies. Yet when the IMF launched its rescue packages in the region, it applied the traditional IMF medicine and even argued, astoundingly, that the problem was that the region's financial markets were insufficiently deregulated. Yet not even a major developed economy, with wholly deregulated financial markets, could survive the same proportional financial shock without similar results; the scale and irrationality of the speculation would have sunk anybody. This was ideological, crooked economic thinking at its worst.

The danger now is that it will rebound not merely on the region but on the world. The Japanese banking system is creaking under the weight of a formidable array of bad debts, with a quarter of all Japanese bank loans now nonperforming. If loans throughout Asia become nonperforming as a consequence of the region's fearfully rapid economic decline, then the situation could become analogous to that of the late 1920s and early 1930s. There will be a regional slump, triggered by the implosion of the banking system, in which every country will be forced into successive but self-defeating rounds of competitive devaluation to attempt to earn the foreign currency needed to stave off default on its international bank debt. Ultimately, though, it will have to default because it does not have the foreign currency earnings.

At the time of this writing, the Chinese have not devalued either their own currency or the Hong Kong dollar, but with the Hong Kong economy sliding into a slump, through lack of confidence and an export contraction, their continued compliance cannot be relied on. Yet if the great Japanese and Hong Kong–based banks are brought down, the impact on the rest of the world's financial system will be formidable.

The derivatives markets, among others, depend upon every participant's being able to settle with its counterpart; but if the major banks go bust, the whole market will implode, spreading losses indiscriminately throughout the world. As in 1929, the losses on speculative financial instruments will spread into the financial heartland, affecting its capacity to continue with good honest-to-god financial transactions, thereby undermining the economy of the whole world.

Galbraith has been warning of this danger for years; a deregulated global financial market heavily dependent upon speculative financial instruments to earn its profits is not a boon but a menace. There have been the storm warnings of companies and banks involved in individual scandals and financial misjudgments that have overwhelmed them; but the warnings have gone unheeded. Now, the market's structures are in danger of overwhelming the world economy. Even if we survive this economic conjuncture, the danger is plain to see—and action needs to be taken. The capacity to speculate needs to be reduced, and an international financial system must be constructed that allows countries more countervailing power to deal with the consequences of violent and destabilizing capital flows. There needs to be an international lender of last resort; the world economy needs to consolidate around fewer currencies, whose interrelationships can be better managed; capital flows need to be more long-term; and global banking institutions need to be more closely regulated and superintended. In short, the world needs to adopt Galbraithian remedies and institutions, and to do so urgently.

Galbraith himself, surveying the scene, must simultaneously be happy at his vindication and sorry that the world has had to arrive at this pass to prove his point. But the collapse of communism, together with the evident inequity and instability of contemporary capitalism, has created circumstances where his ideas and views can be assessed more calmly. At bottom it is a question of values; if we are to humanize and contain capitalism so that it can yield its fruits while minimizing its costs, then the effort must be informed by policymakers, politicians, and economists who themselves believe in trying to do right and be just, and in every human being's right to be respected and heard. Galbraith's legacy is that he is just that economist: a man whose values have shone through all his writing and made it so enduring. It is up to us who share those values to carry on where he will eventually leave off, and to hope that we can live up to a tradition that he has been central in creating.

GALBRAITH IN THE
NEW GILDED AGE

◆

Robert B. Reich

IF NOT the most optimistic social critic of the twentieth century, surely John Kenneth Galbraith has been the most buoyant dismal scientist of our age. Always lurking within American capitalism and society are corrective forces that will serve to put back into balance whatever may temporarily have gone awry. In *American Capitalism: The Concept of Countervailing Power*, published in 1952, he debunked the notion of a perfectly competitive modern economy, but reassured readers nonetheless of the inherent tendency within such a system toward balance among large aggregations of economic power, such as business and labor. Six years later, in *The Affluent Society*, he urged greater attention to the "social balance" between the production of private goods and the supply of public amenities. Rather than scold or admonish, he suggested how much better off we would all find ourselves by embracing the same view. A rational appraisal of our situation surely would yield corrective action.

> By failing to exploit the opportunity to expand public production we are missing opportunities for enjoyment which otherwise we might have had. Presumably a community

can be as well rewarded by buying better schools or better parks as by buying bigger automobiles. By concentrating on the latter rather than the former it is failing to maximize its satisfactions. As with schools in the community, so with public services over the country at large. It is scarcely sensible that we should satisfy our wants in private goods with reckless abundance, while in the case of public goods, on the evidence of the eye, we practice extreme self-denial. So, far from systematically exploiting the opportunities to derive use and pleasure from these services, we do not supply what would keep us out of trouble.[1]

Forty years after these words were written, however, we are unwilling to supply ourselves with what would keep us out of trouble. By some estimates, two thirds of our elementary and secondary schools are in disrepair, and too few of them are providing our children with adequate education. Comfortable movement along public roadways and over bridges now requires the most sophisticated of automobile shock absorbers. Public recreational facilities are fast disappearing. More than one in five of the nation's children lives in poverty —lacking adequate housing, clothing, and nutrition. An ever-growing number and percentage of Americans have no access to health care. Publicly supported basic research is on the wane. After rising throughout the 1960s and 1970s, federal investments in education, infrastructure, and research, as shares of gross domestic product, have continued to fall over the last three administrations. They represented 2.5 percent of GDP in 1981, dropped to 1.7 percent by the time Ronald Reagan left office in 1988, and then to 1.6 percent in 1998—lower than at any time since 1962.[2]

At first blush, this degeneration seems curious. For if

---

1. *The Affluent Society,* Mentor edition, 1958, p. 204.
2. *Federal Budgets of the United States,* various issues.

American society could fairly be described as "affluent" when Galbraith first suggested that the problem of production had been largely overcome, America is now wealthy beyond the imaginations of the early readers of *The Affluent Society*. The nation's gross domestic product in 1960 was $2.26 billion (these and subsequent numbers are adjusted to reflect the purchasing power of a dollar in 1992), and disposable personal income then averaged $8660. By 1996, the GDP had more than tripled, to $6.9 billion, and average disposable income had ballooned to $19,158.[3] Nor, by 1996, was the nation any longer engaged in a Cold War. The Soviet Union had vanished. If Galbraith was correct forty years ago in assuming that America could afford, and thus enjoy, a better social balance, surely the nation can afford a far better balance today. And yet it has grown relatively more miserly. How can this be explained?

When the Cold War officially ended, in 1989, there was a brief debate over how to spend the so-called peace dividend. But then our leaders decided that the more prudent course was to keep most of our military intact, in the event it might still be needed. "We have more will than wallet," intoned George Bush, ruefully. There was rekindled hope for a better social balance when Democrats subsequently took over the White House, in 1993, but the new President and the Democratic Congress concluded that, before we could attend to anything else, the budget deficit must be reduced. We resolved to cut it by half (at the time, it amounted to approximately 4.7 percent of our gross domestic product) before embarking on the social agenda that was the foundation of Bill Clinton's presidential campaign.

3. U.S. Bureau of Economic Analysis, *National Income and Product Accounts of the United States,* Statistical Abstract of the United States, 1997, Tables 692 and 699.

The deficit waned, but the bar was lifted again in 1995, when a Republican Congress, backed by several noted Democrats, threatened a constitutional amendment to balance the budget. In order to forestall such an attempt, the administration postponed the agenda once again until the budget was, in fact, balanced. At this writing, the federal budget is balanced. There are even surpluses. But it appears that the bar has been lifted for a fourth time. We are told that we must first "rescue" Social Security (even though the program could be made fully solvent for the next seventy-five years on the basis of relatively small steps taken now), and that we may then contemplate tax cuts or reductions in the federal debt. Should Congress enact a new tax on tobacco, a portion of the resulting funds may be available for social purposes. But there is no talk of a larger agenda. Social balance is not remotely under consideration.

One part of the explanation lies, I think, in what has happened to incomes during the course of the last two decades. The nation as a whole can easily afford to pay for a better social balance, but most Americans cannot afford to do so. Average incomes have risen, yet averages do not always tell the most revealing story. After all, Ken Galbraith and I have an average height of 5 feet 9 inches. He is very tall, and I am very short. When the distribution of anything becomes widely disparate, talk of "averages" can mislead. So it has come to be with American incomes. At this writing, the United States has the dubious distinction of possessing the most unequal distribution of income among all advanced countries, and inequality has increased here more, and more quickly, than in any comparable nation.

Forty years ago, Galbraith warned liberals not to focus obsessively upon the problem of inequality, lest they lose sight of the more fundamental battle to improve the social balance. This was probably wise advice at the time. The left's long-term fixation on inequality had put it into an ideological bind. Its rhetoric and its programs had suggested a zero-sum contest, in which the less fortunate members of society could do better only at the expense of the more fortunate. In a nation uncomfortable with the idea of class to begin with, and especially in an era when Soviet communism appeared to threaten democracy and freedom, such a preoccupation with inequality was unlikely to gain many converts.

Galbraith reasoned, moreover, that the problem of inequality was fading in any event. Postwar affluence was extending to all social classes.

> The first reason inequality has faded as an issue is, without much question, that it has not been showing the expected tendency to get worse. And thus the Marxian prediction, which earlier in this century seemed so amply confirmed by observation, no longer inspires the same depth of fear. It no longer seems likely that the ownership of the tangible assets of the republic and the disposal of its income will pass into a negligible number of hands despite the approving sentiment of those who would abandon the progressive income tax or widen its present loopholes. Meanwhile there has been a modest reduction in the proportion of disposable income going to those in the very highest income brackets and a very large increase in the proportion accruing to people in the middle and lower brackets. [F]ull employment and upward pressure on wages have increased well-being at the bottom.[4]

The Affluent Society appeared in the midst of a historic shift toward greater equality of income. Between 1950 and 1978, families in the top fifth doubled their incomes, adjusted for

---

4. *The Affluent Society*, p. 75.

inflation. But families in the bottom fifth did even better: their incomes rose by almost 140 percent.[5] "By working together," John F. Kennedy noted a few years after *The Affluent Society* was published, "we have recognized that a rising tide lifts all the boats."[6] Kennedy understated the power of the tide. It was lifting the smallest craft even faster than it was lifting the yachts.

Starting in the late 1970s and continuing through the 1990s, however, the trend reversed itself. The incomes of families in the top fifth rose more than 25 percent, in real terms. But the incomes of the bottom fifth dropped by almost 10 percent, and families in the next-to-poorest fifth experienced a drop of 3 to 5 percent. The median income, which had steadily risen in the three decades after the Second World War, stopped growing. Accordingly, total national income became more concentrated. By 1996 the fortunate fifth commanded 47 percent of it, up from around 40 percent in 1979. The topmost 5 percent took home 20 percent, up from 15 percent in 1979. And the least-fortunate fifth shared less than 5 percent, from around 7 percent in 1979.[7] In short, the American economic tide continued to rise, but it was now lifting only the pleasure craft. The small rowboats were sinking.

Wealth became even more concentrated than income. According to the Federal Reserve Board's triennial survey of consumer wealth, by 1995 the top 1 percent of American households owned almost 39 percent of the total household wealth of the nation. Excluding the value of homes, they owned 47 percent. The top fifth owned 93 percent. It is a fair

---

5. Bureau of the Census, *Current Population Survey,* various issues. All data deflated using CPI-U-XI.

6. Remarks at Muscle Shoals, Alabama. May 18, 1963.

7. *Current Population Survey.*

guess that this trend continued after 1995, as stock market values soared. A majority of Americans owned little or no stock in 1995, because they did not have enough income to buy into the market. According to the same Federal Reserve survey, in 1995 the richest 1 percent held *half* of all outstanding stock and trust equity, almost two thirds of financial securities, and over two thirds of business equity. The top 10 percent owned 82 percent.[8] We can assume that these proportions have remained roughly the same, because the median wage has barely risen, and most Americans still have little or no discretionary savings. With its vast concentrations of income and wealth, the last years of the twentieth century truly mirrored the Gilded Age of a century before.

The rich are now paying more in taxes, to be sure, but they are paying less in taxes as a percentage of their total wealth, or even of their total incomes, than at any time in the postwar era. All levels of government have shifted their sources of revenue in recent years from relatively more progressive ones (taxes on income, property, estate, gift, and capital gains) to more regressive ones (payroll taxes, sales taxes, and legalized gambling). As a result, working middle-class families have been squeezed the hardest. They simply cannot afford to pay for a better social balance.

America as a whole can afford it, because the rich have grown breathlessly wealthier, and *they* can afford it. A progressive wealth tax should not be beyond political imagination. And yet, somehow, it is. Which brings us to the second part of the explanation for why America seems to have become relatively more miserly in recent years, despite the extraordinary affluence of its fortunate members. Simply put,

---

8. Edward N. Wolff, "Recent Trends in the Distribution of Household Wealth," *Journal of Economic Perspectives,* forthcoming.

the public has lost confidence in the capacity of government to act in the public's best interest.

The prevailing cynicism is in stark contrast to the public mood at the time *The Affluent Society* appeared. "In the last half century," wrote Galbraith then, "the power and prestige of the United States government have increased. If only by the process of division, this has diminished the prestige of the power accruing to private wealth."[9] Since those words were written, public confidence in government has steadily diminished. By the late 1960s, with the nation's ill-fated venture in Vietnam, Galbraith himself began to shift ground. His optimism about the "corrective forces" within American society remained undimmed, but he appeared less willing to rely solely upon the public sector as the means of attaining better social balance. In *The New Industrial State* he saw government as part of an industrial "technostructure." Both the large American corporation and the federal bureaucracy constituted a "planning system" possessing a near monopoly on all thought about the structure and purposes of modern society. The only way to break the monopoly was to rely on the intellectual community in general, and "the educational and scientific estate in particular," to assume the responsibilities for political action and leadership.[10]

I will not here attempt to summarize the role of intellectuals during the last two decades of American politics, save to say that Galbraith's hope for intellectual leadership has not borne much fruit. While the "educational and scientific estates" had been vocal opponents of the Vietnam War, in more recent years they have spoken neither consistently nor

9. *The Affluent Society,* p. 76.
10. *The New Industrial State* (Boston: Houghton Mifflin, 1967), p. 393.

convincingly about the perils of a divided society and the importance of attaining a better social balance. Instead, the preoccupations of most members of the academy have grown more specialized and technical. The only discipline that now routinely expresses a normative view of society is economics, but economists as a whole have not exactly distinguished themselves by the breadth of their social vision. By professional training, if not inclination, they tend to overlook the values of community, mutual obligation, and compassion. A theory grounded in rational self-interest may explain much that people do, but it offers only limited guidance for determining what society should try to accomplish.

A significant portion of the less fortunate members of our society, along with much of the working middle class, has given up on politics as anything much more than a spectator sport. Herein lies the central dilemma of our time. There is no possibility for a better social balance unless these groups are actively engaged. Yet the sinews connecting ordinary Americans to national politics are thinning. Money buys time on television, and television advertising extolling a particular candidate or condemning another has supplanted political parties and movements as the central organizing device of American politics. Unintentionally, we have embarked upon a vicious cycle in which politicians must permanently court monied interests in order to raise funds for their next campaign. This courtship, in turn, has disenfranchised a large portion of the electorate that lacks such funds or the will and ability to raise them from others. The disenfranchised thus feel that their votes count for very little, and are prone not to participate in elections. Their failure to participate makes politicians even less sensitive to their needs, thereby confirming what they had all along suspected. The "party of nonvoters" continues to gain adherents.

At bottom, the issue is one of social cohesion. Americans

no longer face the common perils of depression, hot war, or Cold War, which were defining experiences for the generations that reached adulthood in the half century spanning the 1930s to the 1980s. Each of these was a threat to American society and culture. Each was experienced directly or indirectly by virtually all citizens. Under those circumstances, it was not difficult to sense mutual dependence, and conceive of a set of responsibilities, shared by all members, that exacted certain sacrifices for the common good. Today, fewer Americans remember these events or the social bonding that accompanied them. Peace and prosperity are blessings, to be sure, but they do not necessarily pull citizens together in common cause.

Moreover, in the new global economy, those who are more skilled, more talented, or simply wealthier are not as economically dependent on the local or regional economy surrounding them as they once were, and thus have less selfish interest in ensuring that their fellow inhabitants are as productive as possible. Alexis de Tocqueville noted that the better-off Americans he met in his travels of the 1830s invested in their communities because they knew they would reap some of the gains from the resulting growth, in contrast to Europe's traditions of honor and *noblesse oblige.* "The Americans are fond of explaining almost all the actions of their lives by the principle of self-interest rightly understood; they show with complacency how an enlightened regard for themselves constantly prompts them to assist one another and inclines them willingly to sacrifice a portion of their time and property to the welfare of the state."[11] Today, increasingly, the geographic community within which an individual lives is of less consequence to his or her economic well-being. It is now possible to be linked directly by

11. *Democracy in America* (F. Bowen, trans.; New York, 1862), bk. II, ch. 8.

modem and fax to the great financial or commercial centers of the world.

Social cohesion also depends on "it could happen to me" thinking. Social insurance, the public provision of education, roads, and so forth, assume that certain risks and needs are commonly shared. Today's wealthy and poor, however, are likely to have markedly different life experiences. Disparities have grown so large that even though some of the rich (or their children) may become poor and some of the poor (or their progeny) may grow rich, the chances of either occurring are less than they were several decades ago. The wealthy no longer live under a "veil of ignorance" about their futures, to borrow the philosopher John Rawls's felicitous phrase, and they know that any social balance is likely to demand one-sided sacrifice. They will be required to subsidize the poorer.

A final point: people at or near the top, or even in the upper tiers, simply do not see much of the bottom half any longer. Separated geographically, economically, and culturally, the poorer members of society have all but disappeared. The people who produce or talk on the television shows, who write the editorials and columns, and who raise the money for political candidates have no reason to suppose that so many people in this country are still having a hard time of it. Marketers and advertisers do not pay much attention to them because they have little buying power relative to the people in the top half. Pollsters do not pay much attention because they vote far less often. The people they *do* see or attend to are doing just fine, some of them extraordinarily well. And thus it is easy to conclude that everything is going well for everyone, in this new Gilded Age.

Galbraith's analyses typically had happy endings because of his confidence that the "corrective forces" within American society would prevail. His writings of late have evinced less optimism, however. "Books of this genre are expected to have a happy ending," he noted at the end of *The Culture of Contentment,* published in 1992:

> With awareness of what is wrong, the corrective forces of democracy are set in motion. And perhaps they would be now were they in a full democracy—one that embraced the interests and votes of all the citizens . . . Alas, however, we speak here of a democracy of those with the least sense of urgency to correct what is wrong, the best insulation through short-run comfort from what could go wrong. There is special occasion here for sadness—for a sad ending.[12]

An affluent society must rest on a robust civic culture if it is to respond to public needs. Otherwise, private wants dominate all discussion, and the "public interest" is understood to be little more than the sum of such private motivations. There can be no claims based on fairness or social justice, or even on public welfare, because there is no moral community within which such principles have been devised and shared. Thus the dilemma we now face. Neither government officials acting on their own, nor an intellectual elite espousing moral visions, can rejuvenate a civic culture that has atrophied. The ending need not be a sad one. But the quality of leadership now required is greater and more broadly based than it has been at any time during the years since John Kenneth Galbraith first put his formidable pen to paper.

---

12. (Boston: Houghton Mifflin, 1992), p. 174.

KEN GALBRAITH AS
WORLDLY PHILOSOPHER

———————◆———————

Robert Heilbroner

JOHN KENNETH GALBRAITH shares one important mark of distinction with John Maynard Keynes, his only competitor in the field for which both are most widely renowned. It is an aversion to the use of their first names. Anyone calling Maynard Keynes "John" would not have been invited to dinner again. The same for Ken Galbraith,[1] for whom, as with his British rival, "John" is reserved for the covers of his books, not for conversation.

But I can sense a protest in my audience: Ken Galbraith on a par with Maynard Keynes as an economist? Surely that is taking this celebratory occasion too far. But wait! But wait, wait! I did not say that their fame rested on their economic contributions. Indeed, as I see it, in both cases it lies in a much deeper achievement: both men changed the public's attitude toward economics. Somehow, Maynard Keynes conveyed to people, including the millions who never read his books, the idea that the economy, however indispensable,

---

1. EDITOR'S NOTE: Katharine Graham, earlier in this book, explains why this is so for Ken Galbraith.

was also an unreliable and, on occasion, a dangerous component of our society—an element that must be buttressed and reinforced by another that, prior to his influence, was largely regarded with distrust verging on fear. That salvaging instrument was, of course, the government.

Ken Galbraith has taken on a similar task. Although never in opposition to that of Keynes, his objective was aimed at a different aspect of our economy. To the hundreds of thousands who read his books with easy comprehension and deep pleasure, the lesson was that the economy—the vaunted font of the riches of our society—was also a mixture of glitz and neglect. In what is surely the single most quoted passage of *The Affluent Society*, he writes:

> [T]he family which takes its mauve and cerise, air-conditioned, power-steered, and power-braked automobile out for a tour passes through cities that are badly paved, made hideous by litter, blighted buildings, billboards, and posts for wires that should long since have been put underground . . . They picnic on exquisitely packaged food from a portable icebox by a polluted stream and go on to spend the night at a park which is a public menace to health and morals. Just before dozing off on an air mattress, beneath a nylon tent, amid the stench of decaying refuse, they may reflect vaguely on the curious unevenness of their blessings.[2]

I am not sure, today, whether either of these remarkable men can be said to have fully achieved his objective. Keynes's advocacy of an expanded and legitimated role for government won strong support during the Depression-ravaged years in which it was first propounded, up through President

---

2. *The Affluent Society* (Boston: Houghton Mifflin, 1958), pp. 198-199.

Johnson's Great Society. Alas, Keynes's view has lost ground in these more recent years of Galbraithian "affluence," although I think, myself, it must ultimately carry the day, if the day is not to carry us.

Ken Galbraith's influence also hangs in the balance. His target was moral rather than political, although he was far from blind to the root of the problem in sociopolitical realities. But there seems to be some evidence of the lasting effect of his attack on the mix of goods and bads that are the reality of our vaunted multitrillion-dollar gross domestic product, in which *gross* is indeed the right word. A steady flow of books and news-reporting keeps us conscious of the underside of an economy that leads the civilized world in the wealth that accrues to the top, but that trails in its ability to share that wealth with those at the bottom. That awareness cannot be attributed solely to Ken's work, but I think that few would deny the debt owed to it.

In fact, it occurs to me, as I write this assessment of Ken's place in the world as well as in our affections, that it was probably wrong to stress too much his role as a moralist, especially at a time when the world conjures up skepticism more readily than admiration. For an emphasis on morality diverts our attention from his keen analytical eye for the institutional character of modern capitalism, such as his description of the "countervailing power" that lies behind much of its economic dynamics.

Indeed, when I try to assess the full measure of this extraordinary ambassador, administrator, president of the American Economic Association, as well as molder of public opinion, a better description comes to mind. Ken Galbraith is a modern exemplar of what used to be called a political economist— the most influential have been called, I forget by whom, worldly philosophers. In a day in which the word *worldly* raises suspicions, and in which philosophy is regarded as the next best thing for those uneasy with differential calculus, such an accolade may be thought of small worth, but I do not think that Ken will resent being placed with those who share this appellation.

GALBRAITH AND
FRENCH SOCIAL DEMOCRACY

◆————

Michel Rocard

MY GOOD FRIEND J. K. Galbraith has written so much, and on so many subjects, that it is difficult for me to single out what has for me, as a French social democrat, been his greatest contribution.

The major theme running through his work, whether one is looking at his views on money, economic history, development, or on poverty, is without doubt his belief that there can be no successful economy in the absence of market forces, and that the market economy itself would be neither stable nor widely accepted if it did not incorporate a substantial element of social responsibility.

The importance of this message has never been greater than in today's conditions of globalization and wide-ranging deregulation. It is therefore a pleasure, as well as a gesture of devoted friendship, to reflect on those themes on which he has been, for me and for many other Frenchmen of my generation, a master, a destroyer of false gods, and a trailblazer without equal.

But to begin at the beginning. To read Galbraith is always a treat. He is capable of a dry and trenchant wit, a caustic verve, rarely to be seen in the writings of eminent scholars. His lampooning of everything that he finds second-rate or unworthy gladdens the heart with its wholesome mischievousness. And he manages even better, if that were possible, the art of exploding the illogicality or absurdity of the propositions of those who put them forward and who he believes thus deserve to be put down. The few pages that he has devoted in this vein to William Simon, for example, have given more than one reader, if not the person directly concerned, much amusement.

The description, in *Annals of an Abiding Liberal*,[1] of his encounters with the FBI thus has something merciless about it which gives joy and hope to all those who in their lives have had occasion to experience at first hand the unfathomable stupidity of large bureaucracies. And his *A Note on the Psychopathology of the Very Affluent* brings together this gift of sardonic wit, which I admire, and an acuity of purpose that goes a long way beyond mere raillery. It is through this work that Galbraith introduced me to Thorstein Veblen, for which I am very grateful.

His sense of humorous irony can sometimes go far beyond conventional bounds, with the result that he may be quite unpleasant without intending it. I cannot recall at which important academic ceremony the cream of the French intelligentsia in the social sciences had been convened at a meeting presided over by General de Gaulle himself. I am five feet seven inches tall, exactly the average height of my countrymen. In this large gathering our heights varied, but by the same token this added meaning to the concept of average height. De Gaulle and Galbraith exchanged a few words over drinks. And what did they talk about? About how

---

1. (Boston: Houghton Mifflin, 1979).

important it was that the world be ruled only by very tall men . . . I did not compliment him on his democratic tendencies as, despite our intimacy, to do so would have exceeded the bounds of our friendship. But no more of this. Galbraith's mischievous sense of humor should not be commented on, but simply enjoyed.

His contributions to contemporary economic thought are many and important. I should like to mention only two, because I believe them to be key, and because they have helped me to develop and consolidate my beliefs in an area of economics that is not principally mine and in which I lacked the theoretical basis on which to develop and back them up.

The first is the view of the contemporary economy as consisting of two systems. This view is commonplace today, but that was not the case twenty or thirty years ago. I am a French social democrat, a rare species that has been a minority, and possibly is still, and that for decades wallowed in an atmosphere of state socialism and vindictive redistribution. Make the rich pay; take money from wherever it can be found; the bosses are the enemy—these were the devastating slogans that for so long in France were the war cries of a radical unionism that placed more faith in revolutionary political change than in social negotiation. It most certainly reflected the strong and long-felt influence of the Communist Party on society in France, but it was also a commentary on the poverty of ideas of the socialists themselves.

When Lenin seized power in Russia for the Bolsheviks, the Socialist International (the second one, created in 1889, notably by Jean Jaurès) made the right response. It rejected the communist interpretation of socialism by an overwhelming majority and reaffirmed its faith in civil liberty, which it took to be self-evident and not in need of formal definition, in human rights, and in representative democracy. Communist parties were formed by new militant activists, here and there attracting disillusioned socialists, always in a minority. France is unique in that in January 1920 the majority of the Socialist Party of the day decided to establish a Communist Party, bringing with it the nucleus of young militants, the local organizations, what little money they had, and, most important, the newspaper *l'Humanité*.

That is the background to the out-of-dateness of much French thinking and economic perception, in addition to that which can be blamed on our long tradition of centralization. It is why those who were the standard-bearers of socialism in our country, of whom Léon Blum was in the front rank, did not add to their passionate condemnation of Soviet totalitarianism an equally strong disapproval of the vision of state socialism, which social democracy has supported in the past and which the Soviets, however absurd and criminal, had taken to its limits. In his great speech of 1920, in which he spoke of his wish to "stay at home in the old house," Léon Blum nevertheless spoke of a dictatorship of the proletariat.

That is why the Popular Front was able to come to power in 1936 without any kind of economic program, and why it collapsed in the general confusion of a severe financial crisis. After the Second World War, the governments of the Fourth Republic were so weak and so short-lived that it was the upper ranks of the civil service who governed France. Apart from the Algerian question, they did a good job. The priorities and constraints of the immediate postwar years— reconstruction, the infrastructure, exchange controls—all fitted quite well with an intelligent state socialism.

It was only when Gaullism established itself, and the prospect of a conservative government for an indefinite period of time emerged, that the need for the political left in France to rethink its economic ideas began to be keenly felt.

French social democrats, who always disdained thinking of themselves as social democrats on the German or Scandinavian model, then found an elegant way of sidestepping their difficulty in truly accepting the market economy. The shortcut was the European adventure, into which a large majority of us flung ourselves. Peace between France and Germany provided the grounds for neighboring countries and nonextremist political forces to link their economies and then their markets.

And we led the crusade in favor of greater economic realism. I apologize for this historical digression, but it helps to explain why and how John Kenneth Galbraith gave us, somewhat as Keynes had done twenty-five years earlier, certain insights without which we would not have been able to take up and win the challenge. It is thanks to our success that France today has a well-respected and popular social democratic government, a sound currency, a healthy balance of payments, a stock market that does not mistrust government's motives, and, at long last, the beginnings of a downward trend in unemployment.

During the 1960s, the success of the market economy was self-evident. We were in our "thirty glorious years," growth was rapid, and the consumer society was taking hold, at the same time as the failure of communist countries in maintaining living standards was becoming increasingly apparent. The revolutionary challenge to capitalism had begun to lose its way.

The nationalist, redistributive, and state-centered doctrine of the French left became less and less relevant. The party apparatus of the communists and the socialists, and the militant majority bound by this intellectual tradition, fell back on two forms of anticapitalist belligerency. One was the support of the Third World in a denunciation of American imperialism, and the other was the defense of the "small" against the "big" in the developed world. It was a time of vilification of large industrial and commercial holding companies. But for those vital spirits of the socialist left who remained capable of objective thought, these so-called theoretical visions were two blind alleys.

It was around this time that the "affluent society" came about. Galbraith was not alone in seeking to describe and understand this new phase, and many great French economists won fame in the attempt. The most important, without any doubt, was François Perroux. It was Galbraith, however, with his gift for analysis, who was best able to join the separate elements and propositions into a connected, complete, and satisfactory whole.

The market is efficient, and it is pointless to question it. The astonishing period of growth through which we have been living is bound up with the ascendancy of manufacturing. By now the largest enterprises, for which the dual contemporary economy is still only a small cloud on the horizon, have shown that they can free themselves from the market and can control it. The major risk here is growth in corporate debt at a rate higher than growth in output.

And Galbraith stresses that the two main concerns for society emanating from this new social economy are the need for regulation in the public interest and the threat to the environment. He does so with his unique brand of humor:

Cars have an importance greater than the roads on which they are driven. We welcome expansion of telephone services as improving the general well-being but accept curtailment of postal services as signifying necessary economy. We set great store by the increase in private wealth but regret the added outlays for the police force by which it is protected. Vacuum cleaners to ensure clean houses are praiseworthy and essential in our standard of living. Street cleaners to ensure clean streets are an unfortunate expense. Partly as a result, our houses are generally clean and our streets generally filthy.[2]

The Affluent Society is also enlightening to read on the nature of inflationary pressure during a growth period. It is even more so in its steadfast call, subtle but firm, for regulation in the public interest.

Finally, I should like to quote another excerpt whose prophetic nature becomes obvious as soon as one appreciates that this was written in the late 1950s:

> But the car and the aeroplane, versus the space to use them, are merely an exceptionally visible example of a requirement that is pervasive. The more goods people procure, the more packages they discard and the more trash that must be carried away. If the appropriate sanitation services are not provided, the counterpart of increasing opulence will be deepening filth. The greater the wealth, the thicker will be the dirt. This indubitably describes a tendency of our time. As more goods are produced and owned, the greater are the opportunities for fraud, and the more property that must be protected. If the provision of public law enforcement services does not keep pace, the counterpart of increased well-being will, we may be certain, be increased crime.[3]

Step by step, in his books, especially in *American Capitalism: The Concept of Countervailing Power*[4] and *The New Industrial State*,[5] he develops his view of an economic society. Its main

---

2. J. K. Galbraith, *The Affluent Society* (London: Hamilton, 1958), p. 105.
3. Ibid., pp. 198–199.
4. First published in 1952 (London: Hamilton).

attributes are an objective and partly positive view of multinational corporations, and a detailed macroeconomic analysis of the adjustments, dysfunctions, and disequilibria of the two-tier economy in which market forces apply only to those companies too small to influence the market in which they operate.

These intellectual tools enable him to establish the relevance of diagnosis and at the same time to set objectives for political and collective bargaining, regardless of whether these objectives are of a legislative or a contractual nature. All this has been useful to the development of economic ideas throughout the world. If there is one country, however, where this contribution has played a major role in giving a new meaning to trade union strategies and to the political debate, that country is surely France.

An important and relevant subject for debate is this topical question: whether the state should intelligently regulate the market, by giving it a degree of direction and outer limits, rather than leaving it free of all external controls; or whether the state should manage the economy and use its resources to counterbalance enterprises that are big enough not to be subject to market forces.

Another book I should like to acknowledge gratefully is *The Nature of Mass Poverty* (1979). For the past eighteen months I have chaired the European Parliamentary Commission on Development and Cooperation. Our main area of work is Africa. I cannot say how much this book, even though it was written almost twenty years ago and deals mainly with India, has helped me in my present work.

The great strength of Galbraith, in that book as in virtually all his works, is that he never separates economic theories and the data on which they are based, as well as the models

---

5. First published in 1967 (London: Hamilton).

that describe them, from the real world of the men and women whose lives they affect. One could well ask oneself whether, all things considered, is he not, deep down, more a sociologist than an economist.

After having demolished, in his inimitable way, the reasons given for mass poverty—lack of natural resources, bad governance, the greedy rich, the way things are—Galbraith concedes there is a grain of truth in each, but not enough to explain all the circumstances. He then, in an innovative way, formulates his two models: the "equilibrium of poverty," and "accommodation." Once again, his models help to explain measurable economic facts in terms of prevailing behavioral standards. It is this depth of sociological understanding of an economic theory that in my view carries the day.

I do not know whether Galbraith would today defend, as strongly as he did in that book, the notion that urban mass poverty is more bearable and perhaps also less structural than rural poverty. On this point, too, the world has changed in the past twenty years. However, the data available to me, and what I have been able to see for myself, confirm absolutely, even for urban poverty, the notions of an "equilibrium of poverty" and of "accommodation."

It remains true, and Africa illustrates this, that any injection of external resources tends to get diluted and reabsorbed in a way that allows the original situation to re-assert itself. This is why official development aid has produced such poor results. And one sees confirmation each day that living at the edge of famine discourages the taking of any risks, whether economic or technological. Whatever may be the promise of potential gain, the risk of failure, which can be life-threatening, precludes any measures that might otherwise have great chances of success.

These two tragic laws continue to exercise their baneful influence in all known areas of poverty. Galbraith attributes this to a combination of an instinct for survival and cultural barriers, in a way that perpetuates the respect given to the ancient ways of doing things, inherited from tribal forefathers. He concludes persuasively that it is pointless in such circumstances to try, in the name of progress, to address a global population either through education or through technological innovation.

It is the 10 or 15 percent of men and women who are somewhat nonconformist—because of their youth, their courage, and their refusal to accept the status quo or to give up their aspirations—who represent the only hope for the rest of the population to follow their example. But in the meantime, this minority needs our support.

On the question of international ethics, it is not easy to fashion a general rule in line with this principle. But when one knows in detail how things happen in practice, one can better see ways of proceeding without the appearance of differentiation. The initiative must come from the poor, but it is up to the providers of official developmental aid to create or support the conditions in which such an initiative might flourish.

I cannot understand why an analysis carried out in this way has not yet been recognized as being of universal relevance, but I believe it can greatly contribute to an improvement in the results achieved by official aid to developing countries.

In short, my good friend Galbraith has played such a key role in shaping the positive evolution of attitudes and economic perceptions of my generation that I am grateful to have had the opportunity to say to him here, most warmly and sincerely, Merci.

Translated with the assistance of H. Didiot-Cook

JOHN KENNETH GALBRAITH
AND THE MYTHS OF
ECONOMICS

———— ◆ ————

Stephen A. Marglin

G ALBRAITH, as this volume attests, is a man of many parts. A man of letters, a distinguished public servant, he is also one of a handful of truly original and creative thinkers in twentieth-century economics.

THE GALBRAITHIAN ACHIEVEMENT

John Kenneth Galbraith's principal contributions to economics are contained in two landmark books, *The Affluent Society* and *The New Industrial State*. Actually these are one book in two volumes. The first, published in 1958, argues that, for the first time in human history, mid-century America had reached a point where expansion of production no longer needed to be the overwhelming or even the primary concern of society. Increasing consumption served ever more marginal wants and required, as a result, the constant manipulation of the consumer to sustain the expansion of the economy. Hence the continual flow of new products (more often than not little different from the old ones), products relentlessly urged upon us by advertising. By contrast, poverty provides a certain immunity to manipulation—the hungry man knows that it is a loaf of bread and not a new deodorant that will solve his most pressing problem—but poverty, for the first time in history, is the lot of a small minority, not the fundamental reality of the overwhelming majority. (And for this minority a generally rising tide cannot be expected to lift many boats; a brief discussion tucked in at the end of *The Affluent Society* gives the rationale for the specially targeted programs, like Head Start, that under Lyndon Johnson would, a decade later, become the backbone of the Great Society.) Indeed, the social function of growth is no longer to provide the needs of people as consumers, but to finesse two otherwise intractable problems.

First, the problem of the distribution of income. As long as the pie keeps growing, and everybody's piece becomes bigger, we need not fight so much over the relative size of individual slices.

Second, capitalism had not (and has not since) found a way to deal with the problem of unemployment other than to produce an ever-expanding array of goods. Even if the economy no longer requires it, politics and culture require work in return for income—except for the young, the aged, the infirm, and, until the end of "welfare as we know it," mothers of small children. As Saint Paul put it, "He who does not work, neither shall he eat." Or at least not drive the latest model car. So expanding production is a way—indeed, the only politically acceptable way—to expand employment, rather than the other way around.

So long as employment is the chief means of income security for the able-bodied, high and expanding production is a necessary evil. We worship at the altar of production and continue to exalt the captains of industry, not because we need the goods that are the ostensible end product, but because this is the only path to political peace in the age-old conflict over the distribution of the pie between rich and poor and because production, no matter how useless, legitimates income security. Neither income distribution nor income security was a trivial consideration for the generation tried by the ordeal of the Great Depression before its trial by fire in World War II.

This worship of the gods of production is not entirely spontaneous. Galbraith offers a short course in the history of economic thought to show how an economics that originated in the eighteenth and nineteenth centuries has outlived its usefulness. The emphasis on growth that began with Adam Smith suited a period when production was indeed the paramount necessity, but continues to flourish not because it serves the general good but because it admirably promotes the interests of the corporations that produce the goods they work so tirelessly to promote. Myriad pressures to conformity with this "conventional wisdom" (one of the many Galbraithisms that have found their way into common language) allow it not only to survive but to flourish.

This is not, however, without cost, for the cost of private opulence is public squalor. It is the public sector that must provide amenities that cannot in their very nature be commodified. But the public sector is starved for resources, because it threatens the power of the corporation.

John Kenneth Galbraith was not the first to argue that the economy of scarcity was a historical phenomenon rather than the permanent condition of humankind. He cites among his predecessors another John who went by his middle name, John Maynard Keynes. In 1930, Keynes wrote a short essay to alleviate the gloom and doom of the slump that was to become the Great Depression. This essay made the remarkable assertion that the economic problem might be solved in the course of the next hundred years, at least if the economic problem is defined as the satisfaction of "needs that are absolute in the sense that we feel them whatever the situation of our fellow human beings may be"—as distinct from "those which are relative in the sense that we feel them only if their satisfaction lifts us above, makes us feel superior to, our fellows" (1931, p. 365).

The distinction between these two kinds of need, central to Keynes's (and Galbraith's) purposes, has become lost over time, as both kinds are subsumed into consumer preferences; not uncoincidentally, this has happened as absolute needs have come to play less and less of a role in people's consumption.

Keynes differs from Galbraith on two important counts. Galbraith notes one of them: Keynes in 1930 was speculating about a relatively distant future; Galbraith in 1958 was talking about what he regarded as a *fait accompli*.

The second difference is that Keynes foresaw a gradual withering of the economy as more and more people became emancipated from the need for remunerative employment. With this withering would come two possibilities. One was the flowering of human potential that the economic problem had held in check; the other, that eons of conditioning in terms of scarcity might make the vast majority of human beings unfit for the new freedom from economic need. Keynes remained agnostic on how a future without economic compulsion would maintain itself.

Galbraith, a student of politics and sociology as well as of economics, saw more formidable obstacles to this emancipation. His own role was that of a Hegelian muckraker: if freedom is insight into necessity, he would provide the insight that produced the freedom. It would, however, require another volume to do so.

The New Industrial State is one of the books that formed me as an economist. I was already a young assistant professor at Harvard when the book appeared, and during the previous fall had been entrusted with the basic graduate theory course, a course that until then had been the exclusive property of departmental mandarins. I did not take economic theory overly seriously as a descriptive enterprise—it seemed too far-fetched. And in any case my teachers had presented economic theory as operations research, as the logic of constrained maximization, the better to plan the activities of a firm, a government enterprise, or any organization with limited resources. But, this being the 1960s, students were beginning to ask all sorts of questions, including questions about the relevance of economics to the economy. For these I had no answers, even though I could manipulate Jacobian matrices with the best of them.

The New Industrial State explained the irrelevance of the received doctrine, why it survived despite its irrelevance, and—most important—provided an alternative vision of the way the economic world worked. It rounded out the story that *The Affluent Society* had begun by explaining how the producer had evolved from passive respondent to the consumer's wants and needs to active molder of those needs. Some of the pieces in the puzzle had been put in place by others, for example, the transformation of the entrepreneurial corporation to the managerial corporation, from the corporation reflecting a dominant stockholder *à la* John D. Rockefeller, Andrew Carnegie, and Henry Ford, to the corporation whose stock was so widely distributed that no single stockholder or group could wield control, a vacuum into which management itself willingly stepped. Galbraith filled in some important details, for instance, the idea that power was in fact shared by a much wider group of people than fit the notion of management. Power belonged not to top management but to the *technostructure,* a group comprising "all who bring specialized knowledge, talent, or experience to group decision-making. This, not management, is the guiding intelligence—the brain of—the enterprise" (p. 71).

More important, Galbraith provided an overall framework into which to fit the pieces. The argument is sweeping: in the grand march of history, scarcity determines power. In the Middle Ages, land was scarce, so the feudal lord was all powerful. After the Industrial Revolution, capital replaced land as the scarce factor *par excellence.* Hence the power of the capitalist. But the modern corporation, facilitated by the disappearance of the entrepreneur, is able to ensure a steady flow of earnings it can hold on to for investment—there is effectively no group of stockholders in a position to demand the distribution of earnings. So capital is no longer scarce. What has become scarce in the modern world of complex technology, marketing, and planning is the knowledge to assemble raw materials, integrate them into an efficient production process, and—most important of all—prepare the ground for consumers to need the product. The technostructure is the repository of this knowledge and holds the key position in the contemporary economy that the feudal lord held in medieval times or the capitalist after him.

The technostructure, a whole greater than the sum of its parts, is a formidable power, less assailable than the feudal lord or the industrial capitalist. Profit is a concern of the technostructure, but a limited concern. Profit has to be adequate to finance the perks of office and the growth of output, but there is no compulsion to maximize profits. Indeed, where profits and growth may be in conflict, the technostructure can be counted upon to come down firmly on the side of growth.

With *The New Industrial State* to complement *The Affluent Society*, Galbraith now had a coherent picture to offer, the mirror image of received economic doctrine. Instead of sovereign consumers dictating a pattern of production and resource use to passive producers through dollar votes, the economy operated according to a *revised sequence*, in which the process begins with the goals and needs of the technostructure for ever greater production, and the consumer is manipulated to serve the needs of production. Its power resting on the continued importance of production, production of goods ever more marginal as measured by need, as well as production of ever more destructive weapons (we were at the height of the Cold War, remember), the technostructure would have to be overcome or subverted to make any headway in the project of emancipation from the economy of scarcity.

In both *The Affluent Society* and *The New Industrial State* Ken Galbraith is uncharacteristically diffident, if not downright defensive, when it comes to how to change things. The remedies suggested in *The Affluent Society*, perhaps befitting the quiescent 1950s, are surprisingly modest: a graduated system of unemployment compensation (the level of benefits varying directly with the level of unemployment) to begin to break the link between income security and employment, a sales tax to provide a more elastic source of revenue for states and municipalities. These are not proposals that could by any stretch of the imagination lead to a fundamental transformation of society.

The New Industrial State, appearing as the movement against the Vietnam War was gathering strength, takes a more systemic approach. Here Galbraith was clearly influenced by the ability of the scientific community to move its agenda of limiting, if not actually ending, the arms race, and perhaps even more by the radicalization of the university or, more accurately, its students and younger faculty members. The "scientific and educational establishment" (following his Harvard colleague Don Price) became the means to change the system.

Scientists and social scientists within the academic establishment occupied a critical place in the care and feeding of new recruits to the technostructure. This critical position gives the academic establishment a power and influence disproportionate to its numbers, indeed, a power that might be used to subvert the commitment of the technostructure to more and better of ever more useless things.

Galbraith was diffident but never apologetic about the relatively low ratio of cure to diagnosis. It was achievement enough to provide people with clarity about the world around them. Such clarity may not have been a sufficient condition of their liberation, but it was surely necessary.

ASSESSING THE ACHIEVEMENT

How are we, at a distance of thirty and forty years, to assess the Galbraithian achievement? One way would be to look at how well the ideas of *The Affluent Society* and *The New Industrial State* have played out.

Evidently the world has changed considerably since Galbraith wrote the two volumes of his *magnum opus*. In particular, the corporation has changed, and I think there can be little doubt that the technostructure has declined in importance since the 1960s. Not vanished, but declined relative to the wheelers, dealers, and artists of corporate take-overs and make-overs that at midcentury seemed to belong to a bygone era. Bill Gates is a household word of at least equivalent renown as John D. Rockefeller was a century ago. The entrepreneurial corporation, if not dominant, is alive and kicking. The technostructure, as myriad corporate downsizings will attest, is not the safe haven it once was. Nor are managers secure in their tenure, even if the parachutes tend to be more golden the higher the fall.

Today's corporation does not fit neatly into the pattern described in *The New Industrial State*, and it is not difficult to accept that the revised sequence is itself in need of revision. Revision yes, but certainly we should not throw the baby out with the bath water. No revision that will pass muster outside the closed world of economists is going to restore the conventional wisdom that Galbraith so effectively demolished during the third quarter of this century.

In any case, "testing" ideas about the economy by seeing how they have played out over time is a child's game designed more to embarrass and ridicule than to illuminate. When I was a student, the faculty demonstrated tolerance by teaching Karl Marx and political correctness by debunking him. Galbraith is quite right in refusing to play this game with his own predecessors. It is more than enough, he has suggested, to be right for one's own time, without worrying about whether one is in possession of a crystal ball. Indeed, I completely concur with Galbraith in going the next step: problems begin when theory is expected to have a long life in a world in which the only certainty is change. Problems begin when a theory becomes so entrenched, in part at least because it *is* right for its time, that it becomes the conventional wisdom for a later and totally different set of circumstances. Social inquiry differs from natural science because the world we study will not stand still long enough for us to put it under the microscope.

I propose a very different test. To go beyond the mainstream, a theory must go beyond the assumptions of mainstream theory. We should judge Galbraith's achievement by the extent to which he faced these assumptions head on, as well as by the extent to which he failed to challenge the conventional wisdom embodied in the foundational assumptions of economics.

ECONOMIC MYTHS

This will require a detour to examine in some detail these foundational assumptions. On a broad view mainstream economics is the product of four assumptions about human nature—individualism, unlimited wants, self-interest, and rationality. These assumptions are myths in the sense that they are "fiction or half-truth . . . that forms part of the ideology of a society" (*American Heritage Dictionary*, 1991, p. 827).

The myths that underlie economics pose two problems. First, the foundational myths are not recognized for what they are, *assumptions* rather than facts; second, to the extent these assumptions *are* facts, mirrors to reality, they are mirrors to the reality of the modern West. They are historically and culturally constructed ways of being in the world and not a reflection of "human nature," a *universal* way of being that cuts across culture and history.

The first of these assumptions is *individualism*. Individualism is a word to which economics has lent a very special meaning. Economists take the individual as a given, rather than as a work in process, as the ever-changing synthesis of myriad social interactions. In particular, economics sees individuals as unique bundles of preferences, a term that includes everything from taste in dessert to ethical principle. And these preferences are given and unchanging. You might say that for the mainstream economist, the individual is a set of preferences.

The economist's individuals are assumed to be equal in a certain sense, namely, that all individuals are equally *players*, which is to say that all individuals interact on terms of equality. Not necessarily that individuals are equal in endowments of resources, access to goods, or abilities, but that these obvious inequalities do not translate into inequality of power—equality of power is what is meant by the assumption that all individuals are "players." In other words, standard economics has little room for power. (One exception: economics has always recognized, and deplored, the power to set prices enjoyed by a monopolist.)

Add to this a *radical subjectivism*, the assumption that ethical or aesthetic judgments are like tastes in ice cream—just as there is no objective sense in which vanilla can be said to be better than strawberry, so there is nothing to choose between one ethical or aesthetic view and another.

Add as well a large dose of *consequentialism*—acts are to be judged ethically by their consequences, not by the process—roughly, the ends justify the means—and in this concoction we have most of the necessary ingredients for the economist's faith in voluntary exchange as an area exempt from any scrutiny other than the economistic: if Bob and Sally, or General Motors and Joe Smith, agree to a bargain, each must be better off as a result of this trade, and who am I or who are you to say that society might not be better off.

Individualism is one way of being in the world, and arguably the individualistic map can be found everywhere to some degree or other. But the ubiquitousness of the individualistic map does not justify the assumption that individualism reflects human nature: people deploy other maps along with the individualistic map, and the degree to which one map or another dominates varies from place to place and time to time. The peculiarity of economics is that all these other maps are ignored. The individualistic map crowds out all other ways of understanding, and we are left with a caricature of the complexity of individuals and their relationships with one another.

A second myth is the notion of *unlimited wants* and its companion notion of *scarcity*. Unlimited wants and scarcity emerged at the dawn of modernity as structural and systemic, whereas these phenomena possessed an accidental and intermittent quality outside the modern West. Wants became unlimited, scarcity became part of the "human condition" rather than a sometime, episodic experience at the moment that all rivalry got channeled into the economic arena.

Whether rivalry and competition are part of human nature or a cultural construction is not key here. Even if we accept for the sake of argument that rivalry is a universal human trait, the means by which we act out this rivalry vary from society to society and from time to time. Competition may take the form of contests of oratory or song or feats of physical strength, coordination, and courage; rivalry may be acted out through spells and witchcraft. It is peculiarly modern to channel all this rivalry into the economy.

It is also peculiarly modern that scarcity becomes generalized. Particular, isolated, and incommensurable scarcities have characterized human existence since time out of mind. Remember Joseph, who made his name laying up grain against the famine foretold in Pharaoh's dream? But in the modern world we have one big scarcity: Scarcity with a capital S. Scarcity structures our existence: since everything is interconnected, everything is scarce.

How does this interconnection come about? If you are hungry, no amount of silk or jewelry will answer your need. But if the need is to keep up with the Joneses, then goods are much more fungible. That is part of the story, the demand side, so to speak. The other part of the story, the supply side, is the growth in commerce and monetization of the economy, which facilitates the substitution of goods and services for one another. King Midas may have thought he would never have a problem because he would always be able to exchange his gold for other commodities. He was, among other things, simply ahead of his time. In the modern world such exchange takes place all the time.

Finally, scarcity becomes Scarcity because the means become available to alleviate Scarcity. This sounds paradoxical, but Karl Marx and Sigmund Freud separately came up with the same explanation of the paradox, albeit at different levels. Karl Marx once wrote, "Mankind inevitably sets itself only such tasks as it is able to solve" (1970 [1859], p. 21). Freud somewhere made a similar remark about individual people in psychoanalysis (at least so I believe, but I have not been able to locate the place). The point is that not until the engine of production was sufficiently well developed could the genie of Scarcity be let out of the bottle. Not until the conditions were in place to satisfy desire could rivalry be safely channeled into the economy. Only in the seventeenth century did the European economy become sufficiently oriented toward expansion that the demon Scarcity could be tamed by the god Growth.

Self-interest is a third myth, one that compounds with individualism to banish any consideration of duty, obligation, commitment—indeed, all the concepts that would normally enter into a non-economistic characterization of human beings.

In economics, self-interest has become dominant to the point that other ways of being and interacting are ignored, not unlike the way individualism has crowded out other maps of human relationships. (Observe that individualism and self-interest are not the same thing, though they are often run together in economistic discourse. On a broader view of the individual than is characteristic of economics, there is plenty of room for duty, obligation, and the like.) The point is not that self-interest is unique to America at the end of the millennium. This makes no more sense than the economist's assertion that self-interest is the same everywhere. My assertion is rather that the balance between self-interest and other ways of being is very different across time and space, and that economics is obstinately in denial about this variation.

The "self" and "interest" are equally important elements in the notion of self-interest: the self of the self-interested individual is a self like no other, but the notion of interest is no less problematic. Albert Hirschman's work (1977) suggests that a crucial step in the process of legitimating individualism was the eighteenth-century reinterpretation of motivation. Instead of being driven by brute passions—disorderly, destructive, and violent—human beings came to be seen as motivated by interests—rational, calculating, and benign. Arguably, the metamorphosis of passion into interest was important not only for optimizing an economy based on individualism; if human behavior is predictable and law-like, then economics might hope to be a *science*. More on this disaster anon.

The triumph of interest over passion is the triumph of a particular ideology of knowledge, an ideology that came to dominance as an answer to the social disorder accompanying the Reformation, the decay of feudalism and the manorial economy, the rise of capitalism. Economics is committed—and this is the final myth—to a particular theory, or, rather, *ideology*, of *knowledge*, which equates knowledge with what can be known through logical deduction from "self-evident" first principles (like "society is the sum of self-interested individuals"). Knowledge that comes from intuition or authority is in principle suspect unless and until it can be fitted into the system of deduction from first principles. The economist has no room for the knowledge of experience unless it can be codified into a deductive system, a system that elsewhere (Marglin, 1990, 1992, 1996) I have called *episteme* to distinguish it from *techne*, the knowledge of experience.

The difference between *episteme* and *techne* begins with the distinctiveness of their epistemologies. *Episteme* can be loosely identified with rationality. Its particular Western form is knowledge based on logical deduction from self-evident first principles—Euclidean geometry and the Cartesian method perhaps being the canonical exemplars. The Western form of *episteme* thus combines induction and deduction. Induction plays an important role in determining first principles (like the one that parallel lines never meet), and deduction in reaching conclusions at some remove from these first principles (like the Pythagorean theorem).

In contrast with the basis of *episteme* in rationality, the bases of *techne* run the gamut from the authority of recognized masters (and mistresses) to one's own intuition. One way or another, however, experience is of the essence. Opposed to the small steps of *episteme* are both received doctrine and the imaginative leap—the great aha!—which all at once enables one to fit the jigsaw puzzle together. Received doctrines and imaginative leaps are both knowledge of the whole, difficult to break down into parts. In contrast with the analytic nature of *episteme*, *techne* is indecomposable.

Techne is often difficult if not impossible to articulate. It is revealed in production of cloth or creation of a painting or performance of a ritual or a forecast of economic activity, not in textbooks for student weavers, artists, priests, or economists.

The emphasis on self-interest, calculation, and maximization in economics reflects the ideological dominance of *episteme*. The very notion of calculation and maximization is proper to *episteme* and, indeed, incoherent within *techne*. The self-interested individuals of the economist are thus *by assumption* able to calculate, maximize, optimize their way through life. And if individuals do not conform to this pattern, then a crude misapplication of Darwin ensures that they will fall by the wayside (Grewal, 1998).

GALBRAITH MEETS THE MYTHS

These are, in my view, the critical assumptions. That they form the framework for mainstream economics is reasonably clear. Whether they form the framework for the economy is a more controversial issue. Galbraith's brief rests on the contention that, whatever the case formerly, by midcentury these assumptions were in most respects anachronistic as a descriptive framework for understanding the economy.

It would seem to follow that these assumptions had become problematic, for it is only commonsensical that *economics* cannot make assumptions too much at odds with the *economy* if it is to provide a good description of how things are. But even this common sense has been denied by no less an economist than Galbraith's old nemesis Milton Friedman. In Friedman's view, the assumptions don't matter; the proof of the pudding is in the predictions; if a set of assumptions gives good predictions, we need not worry about the accuracy of the assumptions. This is known in the trade as "as if" —consumers act *as if* they were maximizing utility; producers act *as if* they were maximizing profits. (Friedman's view [1953], it should be observed, is still dominant, perhaps not surprising in a discipline whose practitioners still think positivism is the cutting edge of philosophy.)

There are many problems with Friedman's "as if" economics, but one that has gone largely unremarked is that economists are not content to describe, or even to make hypothetical judgments of the kind "If you do X, then Y will follow." (For instance, if you impose rent control, there will be less rental housing available than if markets are allowed to balance demand and supply.) Well before Adam Smith, economists were heavily engaged in constructing society in the image of the discipline. Promoting the virtues of individualism, self-interest, and rationality, convincing us of the centrality of goods and more goods to a meaningful life, economists have, since the seventeenth century (Appleby, 1977), been in the forefront of constructing modernity or, more accurately, the modern West. I have not noticed a slackening in zeal during my own career. The myths of economics are pernicious because they lead to a distortion of our understanding, but more so because they promote a society that impoverishes our lives in the most important dimensions of human relationships even as it provides us with more and more goods in a vain attempt to fill the void.

For this reason, Galbraith's willingness to jettison the foundational myths when they get in the way of understanding also opens up possibilities to reconsider questions that economics has tried to foreclose, questions that go beyond the assumptions of economics to the assumptions of a good and meaningful life. Galbraith expressed the hope, near the end of *The New Industrial State* (p. 353), that "Presidents in the White House, Prime Ministers at 10 Downing Street will be asked whether they have left their city, state, or country more beautiful than before." This hope seems as unlikely to be realized by Bill Clinton or Tony Blair as by George Bush or John Major, not to mention Ronald Reagan or Margaret Thatcher. But as long as there are unconventional thinkers of the Galbraithian mode about, the possibility of constructing a society more in keeping with human needs and potentialities remains open.

Galbraith's take on the economic myths is worth examining in more detail. Galbraith's individuals, clearly, are hardly the givens of standard economic theory. The Galbraithian individual, in sharp contrast to the being who knows his wants, is continually molded by producers who at every turn shape consumer preferences to the needs of production. Neither will Galbraith have any part of the radical subjectivism that renders all wants as equivalent in moral worth. Nor is Galbraith committed to the individualistic map as the only way people navigate the social terrain. The technostructure is, it has been remarked, more than the sum of its parts, and its members willingly embrace the group ethos. It is clear from the description of the technostructure (1967, especially Chapters 6, 11, and 13) that it is better understood as a set of relationships than as a collection of individuals.

The attack on the notion of unlimited wants is, of course, at the heart of *The Affluent Society* and, afterward, *The New Industrial State*. Whereas according a central place to scarcity may have made sense in seventeenth-century England, which for the first time was developing the means to transcend scarcity, this transcendence has in fact been achieved; at this time, a continued emphasis on scarcity serves only the special interests of those whose social and political position is wedded to the continued expansion of production.

Galbraith is at great pains to affirm the limits on self-interest in the corporation and, more particularly, on the part of the technostructure. Even while hoping and working to affect the goals of the technostructure, individuals are more inclined to submit to group goals and ways of doing things. One of these is the perpetuation and aggrandizement of the group, even at the cost of individual perks or corporate profits.

One can at this point quibble. I have for a long time felt that Galbraith overemphasizes Madison Avenue compared with general cultural forces that have molded and continue to mold our consumerist society. One example will serve to illustrate if not to make the point. It is generally recognized that over most of the second half of the twentieth century, cities became increasingly unattractive and undesirable places for living, not to mention for raising a family. The solution, for the winners of the lottery of life, at least, has been escape—to the suburbs or to a vacation house. Suburban homes and country retreats may involve a certain amount of conspicuous consumption, but they are much more: where people lack "voice" to take joint action to solve social problems, individual "exit" may be the only solution (Hirschman, 1970). In a society in which the individualistic map is as prominent as it is in our own, belief in the power of commodities need be neither a form of fetishism nor a form of false consciousness, as Marxists often claim, or a mindless response to the wiles of Madison Avenue, as Galbraith intimates, but a realistic assessment of the available options. The mistaken belief is not that *being* is based on *having*, but that this is the human condition rather than a consequence of the limited range of options available in our society.

I think the implications of this difference in point of view are important, because in my view consumers, while hardly the sovereigns of standard theory, are not as devoid of agency as Galbraith's automatons. On the other hand, broad cultural forces are harder to resist than Madison Avenue. If culture rather than Madison Avenue is the villain, the difference between intrinsic and relative needs becomes less clearcut: we have met the enemy, and he is us, as the comic strip character Pogo declared sometime in the late 1960s. But in the larger scheme of things, this difference of perspective is a second-order one, if not a quibble.

On one count, however, I have more serious reservations. Nowhere in the Galbraith opus am I aware of any doubt being raised about the capacity of the technostructure to carry out the calculation, maximization, and deliberation that underlie planning. Nowhere that I know of is a doubt raised about the ability of the corporation to maximize profits should it choose to do so. Galbraith, in my view, remains too much a child of the Enlightenment to question the ideology of knowledge that informs mainstream economics.

I regard this as an important blind spot. I have nothing against *episteme* as *one* system of knowledge. On the contrary: we would not be human without our command of *episteme*. The problem, rather, is the claim made on behalf of *episteme* that it is *all* of knowledge, from which stems the proclivity to crowd out other, equally important, systems of knowledge. While *episteme* is essential to our humanness, so is *techne*. Indeed, it is our ability to combine *techne* and *episteme* that sets us apart both from other animals and from computers: animals have *techne*, and machines have *episteme*, but only we humans have both. Oliver Sacks's clinical histories (1985) are at once moving as well as entertaining evidence of the grotesque, bizarre, and even tragic distortions of human beings that result from a loss of either *techne* or *episteme*.

Contrary to the modernist view of knowledge, a major obstacle to understanding is the singleminded emphasis on one way of knowing in the knowledge system of economists. In my view, mainstream economics is deeply flawed by an ideology of knowledge that leads both to distortions of understanding and explanation of actual practice as well as to exaggeration of the extent to which informed calculation and maximization is feasible. Descriptive economics incorrectly sees agents as able to maximize at every turn, and prescriptive economics, equally incorrectly, attempts to calculate the incalculable. The methodological error becomes particularly egregious when we must act in the presence of fundamental uncertainty, that is, when we must act without any good idea of the relevant probabilities. An economics based on calculation and maximization cannot deal with uncertainty. It has little to say about how decisions ought to be made when there are no reliable measures of the probabilities associated with alternative courses of action and even less to say about how decisions are actually made.

Rather than critically examine the system of knowledge that forecloses a serious attempt to address uncertainty, economics simply denies uncertainty. For at least a generation now, it has been assumed that uncertainty could be assimilated into a maximizing framework by the device of subjective probabilities. If one is disposed in that direction, it is an easy intellectual step from the fuzziness at the edges of the distinction to the idea that *all* probabilities are personal or subjective in nature. And this indeed is the dominant view in economic theory today. As with utility maximization, it does not matter for the theory whether individuals consciously calculate the subjective probability distributions required by the theory. "As if" behavior, *à la* Milton Friedman, will do just fine.

Under conditions of uncertainty, decision makers do not and cannot mobilize the apparatus of calculation and maximization. Without something to peg probabilities on, economic agents necessarily fall back on quite different methods—on intuition, conventional behavior, authority. In short, agents rely on some mixture of *techne* and *episteme*, not on the pure *episteme* presupposed by maximizing behavior.

Galbraith is thus right to be suspicious about profit maximization as the goal of the enterprise, but he is right for the wrong reason. Agents do not eschew the maximization of profits because they choose to focus on other goals. Rather, agents do not maximize profits because they cannot. The whole project of profit maximization makes no sense under the radical uncertainty in which business operates.

But sauce for the goose is sauce for the gander. If agents cannot maximize profits, neither can they carry out the complex planning exercise that Galbraith attributes to them in their collective guise as the technostructure. For better or worse, the technostructure is simply unable to operate with the deliberation Galbraith assumes.

POLITICS OF KNOWLEDGE

The dominant ideology of knowledge is not only wrong, it is pernicious, justifying as it does a profoundly antidemocratic economics. Economists claim that our discipline is a science, in marked contrast to other disciplines of social inquiry—sociology, politics, anthropology, and so forth. To a great extent this claim rests on an epistemic rigor that enables us to reach Truths (with a capital T) on the same level as the truths of physics, chemistry, and the other natural sciences. Just as one would not wish the criteria for the safe capacity of a bridge to be the subject of politics, so with economic questions like inflation and unemployment. As long as these issues can be billed as economic and *therefore* above politics, economic managers need not be accountable.

The claim that economics is above politics is no idle, academic assertion. How do we explain such anomalies as the independence from any real political accountability of the public official whose importance to the economy is second only to that of the President, in the country that prides itself on being the world's greatest democracy? I have in mind, of course, the independence of the Chairman of the Board of Governors of the Federal Reserve from the normal checks and balances of politics. Galbraith, writing in the 1950s, when the power and prestige of the Fed were at considerably lower ebb than today, suggested (1958, p. 227) that in the first place the Fed's independence was exaggerated and in the second that such independence as the Fed enjoyed was a reflection of "the belief that monetary policy is the highly professional prerogative of the financial community. As such," Galbraith noted archly, "it must be protected from the crude pressures of democratic government." I hardly wish to be accused of minimizing or underestimating the power of Wall Street, but I think that there remains something more of an anomaly than can be explained simply in terms of the power of the banks and their allies. That the Board of Governors and its chairman are accountable neither to the President of the United States nor to the Congress, not to mention the American people, can in my view be understood only in the context of a society in which the idea of economics as a science is well embedded in the public consciousness.

But scientific economics is a hoax, if not a swindle. Monetary policy, like all economic policy, is necessarily political in the sense of being a central function of modern governance, whether it is politicized or not. There are winners and losers from any monetary policy, and it remains the art (what I would call the *techne*) of good policy to balance these gains and losses. One man's politicization is another's democratic politics.

So, perhaps fortunately for the next generation of economists, there remains something to be done. The great work of forging an alternative to the conventional orthodoxy, of which there is no better representative in the twentieth century than John Kenneth Galbraith, still calls us as we approach the twenty-first. The frontier, I think, is the ideology of knowledge and how this interacts with other myths of economics, so brilliantly exposed by Galbraith in the two works I have focused on in this essay. As pygmies standing on the shoulders of *this* giant, we will at least have a good view!

REFERENCES

American Heritage Dictionary, 2nd College Edition (Boston: Houghton Mifflin, 1992).

Appleby, Joyce, *Economic Thought and Ideology in Seventeenth-Century England* (Princeton: Princeton University Press, 1977).

Friedman, Milton, "The Methodology of Positive Economics," in *Essays in Positive Economics* (Chicago: University of Chicago Press, 1953), pp. 3–43.

Galbraith, John Kenneth, *The Affluent Society* (Boston: Houghton Mifflin, 1958).

———, *The New Industrial State* (Boston: Houghton Mifflin, 1967).

Grewal, David, *Optimality and Evolution in Economics: Darwinism in the Study of Firms and Institutions,* Harvard College Senior Honors Thesis, 1998.

Hirschman, Albert, *Exit, Voice, and Loyalty: Responses to Decline in Firms, Organizations, and States* (Cambridge, Mass.: Harvard University Press, 1970).

———, *The Passions and the Interests: Political Arguments for Capitalism Before Its Triumph* (Princeton: Princeton University Press, 1977).

Keynes, John Maynard, "Economic Possibilities for Our Grandchildren," in *Essays in Persuasion* (London: Macmillan, 1931), pp. 358–373. (Originally published in *The Nation* and *Athenaeum,* October 11 and 18, 1930.)

———, *The General Theory of Employment, Interest and Money* (London: Macmillan, 1936).

Marglin, Stephen, "Losing Touch: The Cultural Conditions of Worker Accommodation and Resistance," in F. Apffel-Marglin and S. Marglin (eds.), *Dominating Knowledge: Development, Culture, and Resistance* (Oxford: Clarendon Press, 1990).

———, "Economics as a System of Knowledge" (Cambridge, Mass.: Harvard Institute of Economic Research, Discussion Paper Number 1585, 1992).

———, "Farmers, Seedsmen, and Scientists: Systems of Agriculture and Systems of Knowledge," in F. Apffel-Marglin and S. Marglin (eds.), *Decolonizing Knowledge: From Development to Dialogue* (Oxford: Clarendon Press, 1996).

Marx, Karl, *Contribution to the Critique of Political Economy,* trans. S. Ryazanskaya, ed. M. Dobb (New York: International Publishers [originally published in 1859], 1970).

Sacks, Oliver, *The Man Who Mistook His Wife for a Hat and Other Clinical Tales* (New York: Summit Books, 1985).

GALBRAITH AND THE
ART OF DESCRIPTION

◆

Amartya Sen

O<small>N THE 15</small><small>TH</small> <small>OF OCTOBER</small> 1968, I encountered John Kenneth Galbraith on the ground floor of the Littauer Center, waiting for the elevator. I had just arrived to spend a year at Harvard, on leave from Delhi University, and I was particularly cheered to meet him that day, having seen in the papers that it was his sixtieth birthday. After acknowledging my birthday congratulations, Galbraith said, "I am very puzzled why you think becoming sixty is a subject for congratulation — why is it an achievement?" "Well," I said, "I suppose I really meant best wishes."

"Perhaps you did," said Galbraith, "but you didn't say that, did you? What do you think you could have meant?" "I guess," I said, "I was thinking of the achievements you would not have been able to have if you were cut off very early." "Reason enough," said Galbraith, "to congratulate a person for his achievements, but surely not for longevity which may help those achievements." The elevator mercifully arrived, suspending further critical examination.

I saw Galbraith — and Kitty — a few times more during my 1968–69 visit to Harvard, but came to know them well, indeed very well, only after I moved to Harvard in 1987. When I reflected on it later, that foot-of-the-elevator conversation in 1968 has interest for me that goes well beyond telling me to watch my words; it gave me something of an insight into the passion for, and delight in, critical verity that make John Kenneth Galbraith such a remarkably penetrating observer. The discipline of critical description (including that of scrutiny of what one is seeing, how to make sense of it, what questions to ask in challenging standard habits of thought) is brought out by Galbraith's writings in a wide variety of subjects and has richly contributed to making him one of the most illuminating writers of our time.

There are reasons to think that the art of critical description is vastly underestimated, in the contemporary social sciences in general, and in economics in particular. If one compares the intellectual activities of description, prediction, and prescription, the latter two tend typically to get much more esteem than the former. Indeed, it is not thought to be high praise to say that a piece of writing is descriptive. (Often, for a student's essay, that serves as a prelude to giving a paper a tame B rather than a dazzling A.)

Positive methodology, which has been dominant in economics for a long time, idolizes *prediction* to the exclusion of other activities. (Some years ago, Milton Friedman even tried to convince Paul Samuelson that seeking realism in description was a great mistake.) While it is true that positivists tend to be most skeptical of the status of prescriptive statements, *prescription* as an exercise does get its due from other quarters, if only because of the urgent need to judge policies and to make them. *Description,* in contrast, is the poor sister of the three in the methodological literature, and even when the light shines temporarily on Cinderella, midnight is never far off.

To be sure, what Galbraith has given to predictive and causal economics has been vast and significant, and his writings on prescriptive and normative matters have been very influential. But I believe we would miss something of the greatness of Galbraith if we do not pay special attention to the remarkable importance of critical description in making us understand what is happening around us. There are two issues here. First, predictive and prescriptive analyses are deeply dependent on astute description. Second, the role of illuminating description goes much beyond serving as an input to predictive and prescriptive activities; it is central to understanding the world in which we live.

ON OBSERVING THE ECONOMIC WORLD

In the exercise of richly critical, relevantly pointed, and constantly questioning description, it is hard to match Galbraith's diagnostic skill or the power and reach of his discriminating observation. When, for example, we reflect on Galbraith's much-quoted description of "the affluent society" as one in which people "picnic on exquisitely packaged food from a portable icebox by a polluted stream and go on to spend the night at a park which is a menace to public health and morals," what we primarily see is an insightful and economical description of the nature of the society under observation. It would be a mistake to see it merely as a foundation for prescriptive or predictive statements to come (important though this role ultimately is.) The first and foremost exercise is critical description of the nature of the society that is being observed. And, of course, it would be a bigger mistake still to consider all this to be just fine rhetoric — a possibility that seems to tempt some commentators. The insights offered by this and related observations go well beyond novelty in elocution.

When one thinks about the major contributions in economics that have come from John Kenneth Galbraith, this aspect of his creativity cannot be missed. Whether (to take a few examples from the vast array of subjects to which Galbraith has contributed) we think about the contrast between the private affluence of many and the public penury of all, or the important role of countervailing power in American capitalism, or the special features of the new industrial state, what we get is a discriminating and fruitful understanding of significant phenomena that characterize the contemporary world. How to change them (an exercise that cannot be predictively informed) and what should be done (a judgment that cannot but be prescriptively involved) are dependent on the illumination provided by the descriptive exercise.

INDO-AMERICAN RELATIONS

The same is true of Galbraith's rich writings on India. His extraordinary success as the American ambassador there was, of course, largely a result of his personality and wisdom, but it was also helped a great deal by the perception in India that this was a person who was deeply interested in understanding contemporary India and in trying to make sense of the confusing world that he saw around him. The couple of occasions on which I saw him at the ambassadorial residence, I was struck by how relaxed and inquisitively engaged he and Kitty seemed to be in talking with people they had, mostly, not met before.

Being a successful American ambassador in New Delhi is a hard job, since Indo-American relations have been problematic since the beginning of the Cold War, with an undercurrent of mutual distrust—a distrust that survives today. American officialdom was already very skeptical of Indian politics (and basically uninterested in the difficult — and ultimately successful — commitment to making democracy work in India), and the lines of international alliances were driving India further and further away from America. (Galbraith wrote to President Kennedy in the spring of 1962: "There was never such a drastic misadventure in modern diplomacy as these minor alliances of [John Foster] Dulles.")

One of the oddities of post-independence relations with India is the way the hatchets on both sides of Indo-British relations were rapidly buried (Amritsar and the Bengal famine ceased to be big parts of the postcolonial memory), while America — from which a great deal of friendly support had come in the years of struggle for Indian independence — promptly proceeded to fill the seat of the principal hostile power. The rhetoric of confrontation was stronger than the deeds that actually occurred. (A good illustration of the contrast was the choice of the Calcutta city authorities to rename the street on which the British Council was located Shakespeare Sarani [Street] and calling the corresponding street where the American cultural office was stationed Ho Chi Minh Sarani.) It is in the light of this growing climate of mutual distrust that we have to judge the remarkable popularity of the Galbraiths — the perception that they were, in some sense, above all this.

This is not the occasion to discuss whether Indo-American relations would have gone better had more attention been paid, in Washington and New Delhi, to some of the things that Galbraith was writing about, both in dispatches and in his publications. I think it would have, but that is a bigger subject than I can tackle here. However, in addition to intergovernmental coolness, Indo-American relations at the level of the respective peoples were deeply maimed by mutual ignorance. In a series of long conversations on India and China, conducted by Harold Isaacs in 1958 (published in *Scratches on Our Minds*, MIT Press), with 181 American academics, journalists, government officials, missionaries and church officials, and officials of foundations, social service groups, and political organizations, Isaacs found that the two most widely read writers on India were Rudyard Kipling and Katherine Mayo, the author of the derogatory and poorly written *Mother India*, which Gandhi had described as a "drain inspector's report." While Americans' knowledge of China and its civilization served as a tempering influence even in the hardest days of Sino-American confrontation, and plays a constructive role in easier times now, the absence of any similar knowledge or understanding of Indian civilization and history remains a barrier to good Indo-American relations today, reinforcing the neglect at the official level.

In Galbraith's perceptive and illuminating writings on Indian culture, in the field of fine arts as well as on contemporary social, political, and economic problems, there is a wealth of material that can make a great contribution to mutual understanding and political engagement. His extraordinary skill at going straight at the major issues — variously neglected in both India and the United States — makes his writings on India so powerful and far-reaching.

On a different and more general issue, the interpretation of Indian civilization has been overwhelmed in dominant Western perceptions by unifocal attention of one kind or another, with India seen either as a wonderland of spiritual wisdom or as a country of unspeakable customs and practices.

Descriptive richness is the quality that is most missed. No one fills this gap better than Galbraith. The consistently friendly yet totally unillusioned attempt to comprehend what is going on provides an understanding that is hard to match.

Joan Robinson, the Cambridge economist, had remarked, after some frustration in trying to size up India, "Whatever you can say truthfully about India, the opposite is also true." Among contemporary writers on India, it is John Kenneth Galbraith who probably deals best with this conundrum. He has been able to do it because of his passion for and skill in descriptive richness and accuracy that are characteristic of his discipline of observation. Illumination through far-reaching, scrutinized description is a territory in which Galbraith has few peers.

EARLY INFLUENCES ON GALBRAITH'S WORLDVIEW AND ECONOMICS

◆

Richard Parker

One of the most important and difficult
of the responsibilities of the economist is
to resist the authority of the accepted.
— John Kenneth Galbraith,
American Capitalism

For those who believe that "the Market" is now everywhere and will forever be triumphant, and that the supremacy of economists is permanently installed in the pantheon of social science, a reminder of history's endless vagaries is in order. In the mid-1950s, an earlier generation also thought it was entering a "new" era. American economists confidently began to speak of unprecedented material affluence based on a new "economic mainstream," an idea whose appeal spread with astonishing speed to a larger public, including America's political leaders and pundits.

This new mainstream, by using freshly evolved techniques of Keynesian macromanagement, plus mathematical advances that included game theory, econometrics, sophisticated regression analysis, and computer-based modeling, had, these economists proclaimed, finally achieved an almost physics-like certainty for the dismal science. More important, these mainstream achievements promised something that had only recently seemed unimaginable: a stable, widely distributed, and virtually unending prosperity for America and, in due course, for the world.

Much has been written about how that earlier Golden Age of economics disappeared. But amidst its original triumphal celebration, no person was more audible and skeptical of his profession's newfound confidence — or indeed the Market's omniscient powers — than John Kenneth Galbraith.

But what gave Galbraith the foresight and skepticism that so many of his colleagues lacked? What was it about Galbraith's background, academic or personal, that allowed him to remain cautionary and independent while others rushed to consensus? Because others in this volume will elaborate on Galbraith's views about the structure and characteristics of modern economic life, as well as his place in the economics profession, I have chosen to comment on a little-remarked dimension of his career: some of the roots and other contributing factors to his thinking and worldview.

In Galbraith, whose originality uniquely synthesizes and draws on elements of earlier economic thought, such a quest is not without danger. But it does have its rewards if it helps us to understand the enduring concerns and arguments that connect the past through Galbraith to our own lives.

Galbraith himself has frequently acknowledged how greatly he was influenced by both John Maynard Keynes and Thorstein Veblen, a view that seems patently true not only by his own admission, but also by a cursory reading of his major works. However, I prefer here to draw attention to two other influences less noted but, I believe, no less significant. The first is a now rather forgotten, once highly divisive debate among American economists that was in full swing when Galbraith was young. The second is a quite intimate connection about which Galbraith has written little: the influence of his father, Archie Galbraith, and the legacy of his politics and worldview.

One striking event will perhaps best capture the divisions that split American economics in the years before Keynes, divisions that deeply affected Galbraith's thinking. Eighty years ago, in late December 1918, barely a month after the Armistice ending World War I, the American Economic Association gathered in Richmond, Virginia. It was the group's thirty-fourth annual meeting, and Professor Irving Fisher of Yale University was its newly elected president.

Fisher remains even today one of the great figures in American economics; Paul Samuelson has called him America's greatest mathematical economist of the pre–World War II era. Fisher gave us the modern Quantity Theory of Money, served as cofounder and first president of the Econometric Society, and was widely recognized in his time as one of the nation's leading social scientists, sought after by colleagues, journalists, and statesmen alike for his views on economic affairs.

For more than a decade, Fisher had been aware of the deep divisions that had troubled the AEA since its founding, in 1885. Nowadays, few students new to economics ever hear of these fissures. The standard text still prefers to emphasize the mainstream's historical continuity, however tattered, and to proclaim the history of economics a broad, steadily flow-ing, scientific progress that descends from Adam Smith down through Ricardo and Mill, to Marshall and Keynes, and then through the 1970s' "rebirth" of microeconomics, to the present triumph of "markets" and "market economics" worldwide.

But in 1918, the gaps within the profession—to say nothing of the world—loomed large, and Fisher, as the AEA's new president, was proposing that he and his colleagues do something about them. The central gap, he explained to an audience who knew full well what he was referring to, concerned the divided loyalties of American economists to the "English" and the "German" traditions.

Fisher's fundamental allegiance was to the English tradition. This was deductive, axiomatic, and used mathematical modeling; it portrayed itself then, as now, as the one "true" economics. To Fisher, "English" meant the world of Smith's pin factory, where both visible and invisible hands toiled, Ricardo's comparative advantage, and Marshall's emphasis on the calculus as method, equilibrium as end state, and the rational maximizing of "economic man" as the formal and necessary foundations of all sound economic thought.

But as Fisher reminded his listeners, the AEA itself owed its existence to the German tradition, brought back to America by young graduate students in economics who had chosen to study on the Continent in the 1880s and 1890s, at a time when American universities granted fewer than a hundred Ph.D.s in economics.

In Germany, these young Americans had seen Bismarck's state at work. They had observed its dynamic role in unifying and modernizing the young nation, and had seen its leadership producing Europe's first real rival to England's unmatched hegemony over the Industrial Age.

The German academic economic style was characteristically

nonaxiomatic and nondeductive; instead, it was empirical, statistical, historical, and intimately concerned with the economic implications of the observable institutions, laws, customs, and habits of the societies in which this new industrial revolution was taking place.

Moreover, in contrast to England's traditions of laissez-faire and often brutally Darwinist economic and social policies, the German tradition had a decidedly "progressive" bent. Its protagonists encouraged the rapid growth of trade unions, agricultural cooperatives, and manufacturing and trade associations (including cartels); helped construct the modern world's earliest social welfare state; promoted the university-based sciences as a research arm of industry; and stoutly defended giving the government itself a powerful hand in shaping the growth of the nation and its economy.

In American economic thought, Fisher claimed, these competing worldviews had reformed themselves into what he called "conservative" and "radical" theoretical camps; a "liberal" camp, oddly, wasn't mentioned by Fisher. The conservative camp, he noted, everywhere and always preferred the refinements of abstract theory, distrusted government intervention, and barely abided the idea of trade unions, cooperatives, the welfare state, or managed trade. The radicals, by contrast, saw economics first as an instrument of a normative and moral "public good." They agitated against their own era of "limited government," attacked concentrated market power as well as income and wealth maldistribution, and sought to advance public policy as a regulator of private economic actions. They regularly chided conservative English colleagues for overemphasizing mathematical elegance over real-world measures of existing economic and social conditions.

Far from barely surviving at the "fringe" of an erstwhile English mainstream of the day, this German tradition was vitally alive and competitive. Indeed, Fisher's address cautiously named no names, its author knowing full well that among his audience that December night were a number of the men who embodied the radical or German tradition that so discomfited him.

Richard Ely, perhaps its foremost apostle and chief founder of the AEA, was there. For years Ely had been a towering figure at the University of Wisconsin, where he had crafted his department into a "brain trust" for Robert LaFollette's progressive Wisconsin Experiment, long before Raymond Moley and Rexford Tugwell had done the same for Roosevelt. Moreover, Ely was also the author of the country's best-selling economics textbook, a position it held for more than three decades.

Ely's younger colleague at Wisconsin, John R. Commons, a seminal figure in American labor economics who was barely less prominent, also sat listening to Fisher. A few rows away from Commons sat Wesley Mitchell, an equally towering figure among a new generation of economists, who, as America's high priest of business-cycle theory, was about to found the National Bureau of Economic Research, still one of the profession's stellar research centers.

Kenneth Galbraith, only ten years old at the time and living with his family on a farm in southern Ontario, was not, of course, in Richmond that night. Nor had he ever heard of Fisher, the AEA, or of the German-English divide. But more than a decade later, as a young graduate student at Berkeley, he would find himself deeply influenced by teachers such as Leo Rogin, who found little favor with Fisher's conservative tradition. And by 1934, when he began his career at Harvard as a young instructor, Galbraith was already beginning to display attitudes toward his departmental elders' conventional marginalist assumptions (and its English tradition) that owed far less to Keynes than to the older and better-established German tradition in American economics.

In fact, when one examines Galbraith's early professional writing from the 1930s and 1940s, the tracelines of this German tradition are visible throughout it. His earliest book, *Modern Competition and Business Policy,* is nothing if not a paean to that tradition's pre-Keynesian assumptions, as are his earliest professional articles in a number of striking ways. None shows any discernible Keynesian or Veblenian influences even after 1936, when Galbraith claims to have been "transformed" by reading Keynes's newly published *General Theory,* or indeed until quite late in the 1940s. Whether the subject is monopoly power and pricing, the role of public works in stimulating growth, or America's postwar economic prospects, it is foremost the echoes of America's earlier German tradition that we hear.

AGRICULTURAL ECONOMICS AND JOHN D. BLACK

It is important to note that a number of Galbraith's early and formative articles were coauthored with his Harvard mentor John D. Black, the great agricultural economist. Long before Keynes wrote *The General Theory* and, in a sense, gave economics a particular — though ultimately unstable — solution to the gap that divided the German and English traditions, the steady erosion of the American farm sector had prompted many agricultural economists and leaders to reject much of Fisher's English tradition.

As Galbraith has written, the Great Depression did not strike American agriculture with novel destructive force, but rather as the latest and the worst in a series of seemingly inescapable miseries. Throughout the 1920s, Galbraith has reminded us, "competing with undifferentiated products in purely competitive markets with costs and prices that none controlled, farmers represented the closest approach to the classical ideal of the economic system," and, farther on, "they were also, of all producers, the most at odds with the system."

As a result, years before the New Deal effectively became the model for a new activist and interventionist government, and well before Keynes provided an economic theory to justify government's macroeconomic purpose, Black and other progressive agricultural economists had sought to escape the English tradition in its classical guise and embrace precisely those activist, pragmatic, and publicly led conceptions of economics that Fisher in 1918 dubbed radical or German.

Black, perhaps significantly, had earned his Ph.D. at Wisconsin, where he had studied under two of the great German-trained economists, Ely and Commons. Galbraith has stressed, however, that even before he himself came to Harvard and fell under Black's powerful sway, his upbringing on his father's Ontario farm was crucial to his formulating the broad set of attitudes that would eventually shape his mature economic views.

"Because of my rural background and study of agricultural economics in particular," Galbraith said, he did not accept what Fisher called the English tradition—a term, incidentally, that Galbraith never uses. Indeed, it was Galbraith's direct experience, mediated by the tradition he was then absorbing, that would instill in him, as he would later write, the belief that, "left to themselves, economic forces do not work out for the best except for the powerful."

But what was this rural background that so influenced the young economist and left the indelible attitudes that later, as a mature thinker, he sought to use Keynes, Veblen, and his own original critique to defend and elaborate?

In both his memoirs and in *The Scotch*, his affectionate and often poetic memoir of growing up in the self-contained world of Scotch immigrant farmers in southern Ontario, Galbraith has described a childhood distant from any noticeable sense of the rural economic deprivation and suffering that haunted so many millions of farmers in those years.

Iona Station, the little hamlet where Galbraith was born and raised, and the surrounding Elgin County, had been first settled by these Scotch immigrants in the 1820s and 1830s. Over the course of several generations, they had transformed rather mediocre soil into comfortable farms of a hundred to two hundred acres. They had accomplished this by hard work, which gave them decent livings from mixed farming that included tobacco, corn, hay, and cattle. There were few who were poor or rich in this community; most were freeholders rather than tenants, and a substantial number had paid off their farm mortgages early in their working lives.

Amidst the Camerons, McPhails, McFarlanes, McKillops, and the like, the Galbraiths were, as Kenneth Galbraith himself describes his clan, "men of standing." "The Galbraiths were regarded, we believed rightly, as being more intelligent than others," he notes in *A Life in Our Times*. "We were also modestly more affluent. Many of our neighbors did not know their position on major political and other issues — the practical benefits of lower tariffs, cooperative buying of fertilizer or binder twine, and the provincial highway system or the case against going to the trenches in World War I—until they heard my father provide it."

One might here imagine that we are seeing a father through the lens of a son's pride, perhaps exaggerated by memory and affection. But when Galbraith's father died, in 1938, the local paper carried a lengthy obituary that testified to the father's enormous influence and standing in the community. The funeral service itself offered such testimony. More than six hundred people attended, in the midst of a raging midwinter Canadian storm. According to the paper, one man, when his car was stranded by snowdrifts, hired a farmer's sled and team to haul the car and its occupants the last six miles to the church.

But who was Archie Galbraith, and why did he hold such an admired and influential place in his community and in his son's life? Galbraith provides only a brief sketch in his memoirs: "My father, a former teacher who never fully rejected that profession, headed a cooperative insurance company that he had helped to organize (as he had once helped organize the first telephone service in the neighborhood) and was a moderately well compensated township and county official," serving as auditor for both town and county even while simultaneously running the family farm.

Archie Galbraith, in addition to his civic role, was also an active local political figure and for most of his life a devoted senior official in the county branch of the Canadian Liberal Party. The Scotch of Ontario had, as a group, been straight-ticket Liberals for much of the early part of this century, influenced not only by a preference for the party members' modestly progressive views, but by their enduring dislike for the Anglo-Canadian–dominated Conservative Party, a feeling stemming, in no small measure, from their collective memories of Tory England's treatment of their ethnic ancestors.

Galbraith remembers quite vividly traveling, as a young boy, about the county at election time and listening as his father pressed for voters' support of whoever happened to be the Liberal Party candidate of the moment. He has often retold the story of his father striding before a crowd gathered in a neighbor's barnyard and mounting a large manure pile. Galbraith says his father called for silence from the surprised onlookers, then with a straight face (but a twinkle in his eye), "apologized with ill-concealed sincerity for speaking from the Tory platform."

Apart from signaling a hereditary element to his son's famous wit, the scene tells us much about the strength of the father's partisan commitments. But during World War I, that loyalty was put to the severest of tests. As members of the British Empire, Canadians had at first loyally rushed forward to serve the Allied cause. But when the casualties mounted horrifically—68,000 out of 242,000 soldiers from Ontario alone were missing, wounded, or dead by war's end—the Canadian government had been forced to turn to conscription, and found itself facing bitter opposition from millions of its own supporters, including Archie Galbraith.

One historian has called the crucial 1917 election, which turned into a plebiscite on the war itself, "the bitterest campaign in Canadian history." In Elgin County, Archie's views were clear: he was already serving as the local draft board chairman, the better to defer more local boys. But the strains on his Liberal loyalties were now deeply visible. Even before the war's end, he and others like him in Ontario began to set out a new political course.

Within months after Irving Fisher tried vainly to heal the great divisions in American economics, Ontario suddenly erupted, producing its own political divisions. Bolting the Liberal Party by the thousands, Ontario voters, including a heavy majority in Elgin County that included Kenneth Galbraith's father and mother, created a new third party: the United Farmers of Ontario.

The new party was led by E. C. Drury, a forty-six-year-old farmer and Liberal Party figure who almost overnight found himself Premier of Ontario. Quickly forming a coalition with the nascent Labour Party, which had simultaneously galvanized thousands of urban working-class voters, Drury's government horrified the Canadian political establishment. Some stalwart conservative leaders claimed to see Bolshevik or even Sinn Fein backing to the movement. No less darkly, under the circumstances, the province's Lieutenant Governor, Sir John Hendrie, denounced the new government as "a move away from party representation toward class warfare."

The new government swiftly enacted what Drury himself called such "a program of social legislation as Ontario and indeed all Canada and North America has never seen, or perhaps thought possible." Minimum-wage laws for women, expanded welfare for widows and orphans, civil service pensions, workers' compensation reforms, new taxes on corporations and utilities, new public savings banks, new credits for farmers and cooperatives, rural road and rail construction programs, giant public hydroelectric projects—all were passed and signed into law in a torrent of governmental activism in less than four years.

But in 1923, the government fell over a difference between its rural and urban partners that was centered on prohibition. The farm community was for it, the workers weren't, and a new Conservative administration was ushered in. With Drury back on his farm, the United Farmers spiraled downward into political oblivion as suddenly as they had risen.

For the Galbraiths, political defeat commingled that year with family tragedy. Kenneth's mother died suddenly at forty-nine from heart failure, just days after her son's fifteenth birthday. Archie Galbraith was devastated and, according to his daughter, seemed "lost" for almost two years afterward.

If Kenneth Galbraith suffered deeply from his mother's death, the tragedy gradually brought him closer to his father. Six years later, when he left Ontario for graduate work at Berkeley, he and his father started exchanging almost weekly letters. In 1934, when Galbraith began teaching at Harvard, and up to Archie's sudden death in 1938, the letters continued. Although Galbraith has never spoken of them, according to his sister, the correspondence was lively and filled not only with local news, but regular and energetic discussions of politics and economics.

Archie, after Drury's defeat, gradually drifted back to his old allegiance and prominent local role in the Liberal Party, but his experience with the United Farmers never left him. In 1934, a rising young Liberal star named Mitchell Hepburn ran for Ontario's premiership on a platform almost as progressive as Drury's. Archie Galbraith was crucially responsible for sending him on to Parliament and eventually the premiership. Hepburn, however, despite controlling a 66–23 legislative majority, proved a disastrous failure and a bitter personal disappointment to Archie.

Years later, in a clear echo of his father's strong ideals, Galbraith — by now an equally devoted Democrat — would find himself torn between party loyalty and the Vietnam War. He would also ultimately choose not only to stand against both the war and his party's leaders, but to help lead a breakaway presidential campaign for Eugene McCarthy and, four years later, serve in George McGovern's campaign. Whether one sees in Galbraith's economic vision and voice the enduring influence of the strong father can surely be debated, but in striking ways it seems no less likely a core foundation.

From this necessarily brief sketch, one ought not to conclude that a once-bitter fight among economists over "German" and "English" directions, or its influences on agricultural economics, or a father's example alone "explain" Galbraithian thought. Yet, I would argue, they give us a deeper understanding of how a young Canadian farm boy grew up to become, as Harvard Dean Henry Rosovsky once described Ken Galbraith, "Harvard's most famous professor." What he did with those influences is entirely Galbraithian; yet by understanding better that he, like other original thinkers in this or any other field, wasn't simply *sui generis,* we can better grasp why, far from standing outside an erstwhile professional mainstream, he has helped advance, sustain, and pass on to us humanity's deepest stream: the quest to use reason for justice and to create a world of plenty, where lives are lived without the scarce supply of any human need.

GALBRAITH
ON GALBRAITH

◆

Andrea Williams

In THE PRECEDING PAGES there have been views of John Kenneth Galbraith from many who know him best, who have seen him as economist, writer, diplomat, political provocateur, art historian, friend, or family member. But what would he say of himself? That may be more difficult, for all know that the intensely personal, the intimate revelation, the sentimental reminiscence are not his preference or his style. As he says in one of the quotes that follow, "I have always tried for a measure of detachment. I've felt that one should hold some part of one's self in reserve."

Luckily, Galbraith has revealed more than he knew in both his fiction and his nonfiction: how his boyhood on a farm altered forever his view of work; what his forebears, the Scotch of Ontario, taught him about social behavior and even religion; of which academic institutions he was most fond and the rules of academic behavior they taught him; what he thought of economics and economists, writing, and politics, the three principal occupations of his life, each of which came with rules of its own; what he thought about family, cherished places, and, finally, his reflections on the wisdom of age. He rarely speaks in the first person, but there is no doubt whose words you are reading and whose voice you are hearing. This is a man of humor and tolerance, not averse to self-enhancement but just as apt to be unexpectedly self-deprecating. The interests in his life are many, his limitations few, for he has been blessed with energy, optimism, and the discrimination to know what suits him best. He is Scotch by ethnic background, academic by preference, social democrat by choice, a magnificent writer and wit by good fortune (and hard work), and what Dr. Johnson used as the ultimate accolade, a Man of Sense.

Here is Galbraith on Galbraith. (The full book titles are on the last page.)

FARMING

My legacy was the inherent insecurity of the farm-reared boy in combination with an aggressive feeling that I owed it to all I encountered to make them better informed. A more commonplace consequence of an early exposure to agriculture is a deeply valid appreciation of the nature of manual labor. It leaves all of minimal sensitivity with an enduring knowledge of its unpleasantness, A long day following a plodding, increasingly reluctant team behind a harrow endlessly back and forth over the uninspiring Ontario terrain persuaded one that all other work was easy. This early life could hardly have been in greater contrast with life at Harvard, where more than six hours of teaching a week is often considered a grave impairment of academic freedom. Regularly since coming to the university, I have been approached at the Faculty Club, on social occasions, and even in the Yard by colleagues who, with an unconvincingly worried look, have said, "Ken, aren't you working too hard?" There was a book last year, another in prospect, my teaching, something in politics. Back of the query lies their natural concern for the union rules. Only with difficulty have I suppressed my reply: "The trouble with you, my friend, is that you've never worked on a farm." (ALIOT, pp. 3–4.)

THE SCOTCH

The decisive source of esteem [among the Scotch], the obverse of that which led to exclusion for ignorance, was information and the ability and willingness to put it to sensible use. This was, by all odds, the most admired trait . . . [E]ducation was only important if combined with good sense . . . The Scotch expected a man to prove his wisdom by putting it to useful purpose. (TS, p. 55.)

In Upper Canada (now Ontario) in the last century . . . there was a moral and political cleavage between the rural Scotch and the prestigious Toryism of the English-oriented ruling class. The resulting attitudes were far from dead in my youth; they required that one be compulsively against any self-satisfied elite. One never joined, and one never overlooked any righteous opportunity to oppose or, if opportunity presented, to infuriate. No psychic disorder could be more useful. It forces one automatically to question the most pompously exchanged clichés of the corporate executives, the most confidently vacuous voices on military adventure, and the most generally admired triteness on foreign policy. To me it has been valuable, I believe, on matters as diverse as the deeply sanctioned obsolescence of neoclassical economics and the greatly self-approving commitment in Vietnam. (ALIOT, p. 246.)

◆　◆　◆

If a man didn't make sense, the Scotch felt it was misplaced politeness to try to keep him from knowing it. Better that he be aware of his reputation, for this would encourage reticence, which goes well with stupidity. And there is advantage in having the unwary and undiscriminating on notice. The Scotch were strikingly immune to demagogy. One reason was the total lack of hesitation in ascribing ignorance to demagogues. Potential followers were warned from the outset.

As a small personal footnote, I have never thought the practice of the Scotch in this respect entirely wrong. As a result I have rarely managed to avoid telling the intellectually obtuse what I feel they ought to know. Even when I have remained silent, I have usually succeeded in conveying an impression. It shows the influence of upbringing. It is not a formula for personal popularity or political success, and, for a diplomat, it can complicate relations with the State Department. (TS, pp. 51–52.)

As many people expect a woman to love men without being a nymphomaniac, so the Scotch expected a man to love money without being a miser. (TS, p. 29.)

Perhaps the fear of enjoying this life too much intruded. A central instruction of our Covenanted (Old School) Baptist Church of Wallacetown, Ontario, was that man achieved grace by eschewing enjoyment for himself and so far as might be possible for others. (ALIOT, p. 444.)

The superior confidence which people repose in the tall man is well merited. Being tall, he is more visible than other men, and being more visible, he is much more closely watched. In consequence, his behavior is far better than that of smaller men. (TS, pp. 53–54.)

My life has been spent in greater or less communion with five centers of higher learning, as that term, often loosely, is used. Two of these, Guelph and Princeton—respectively the least and the most aristocratic in tendency—did not engage my affection. Two, the University of California at Berkeley and the University of Cambridge, I greatly loved. Harvard, where I've spent most of my life, does not lend itself easily to classification. In all five universities, as they all now are, I suffered from a problem in personal relations that I never quite overcame. This was not so much from being more versatile, more diligent, or perhaps more able than my colleagues. Such can be tolerated. The damage arose from my fear, which I earlier indicated and which I never quite suppressed, that my superiority would not be recognized. (ALIOT, p. 18.)

The two academic institutions that engaged my affection, Berkeley and the University of Cambridge, could have done so partly because of their beauty. Cambridge, England— Trinity Great Court, the Wren Library, King's Chapel, the other more intimate quadrangles, the Backs—has no equal in Europe, and certainly not in the spring, when first the crocuses and then the daffodils cover great stretches of field and lawn . . . One learns also at Cambridge how architecture has declined geometrically in taste and excellence—by roughly half in each century since the first Elizabeth. There, much is good because so little is new. (ALIOT, p. 20.)

RULES OF ACADEMIC LIFE

Agricultural economics left me with the strong feeling that social science should be tested by its usefulness. This, as Veb-

164 • BETWEEN FRIENDS

len urged, is a considerable professional handicap. The economists who are most highly regarded in their own time have almost always been those who confined themselves to abstract speculation unmarred by social purpose. (ALIOT, p. 27.)

Scholarship in the social sciences is assessed by its depth and precision but also by the length of time it has required. A quickly completed job, regardless of quality, is bad. A five-year effort is good *per se*. A lifetime work, not quite finished at death, is superb. (ALIOT, p. 60.)

Just as it is understood at the modern university that any idea can be compressed or expanded into fifty-five minutes, so it is also believed that all knowledge on a subject can be covered in either thirteen or twenty-six weeks. (ATP, p. 89.)

[T]here is something cowardly in trying to protect oneself against every eventuality. The university professor who thinks deeply of how to secure his own future regularly ends up thinking of nothing else. (AJ, p. 12.)

Discussion, in all higher education, is the vacuum which is used to fill a vacuum. (ALIOT, p. 27.)

ECONOMICS AND ECONOMISTS

Never forget, dear boy, that academic distinction in economics is not to be had from giving a clear account of how the world works. Keynes knew that; had he made his *General Theory* completely comprehensible, it would have been ignored. Economists value most the colleague whom they most struggle to understand. The pride they feel in eventually succeeding leads to admiration for the man who set them so difficult a task. And anyone who cannot be understood at all will be especially admired. All will want to give the impression that they have penetrated his mystification. This accords him a standing above all others. (ATP, p. 50.)

Economics is not durable truth; it requires continuous revision and accommodation. Nearly all its error is from those who cannot change. (ALIOT, p. 125.)

[R]eputable, or, as it is often called, mainstream economics has for some centuries given grace and acceptability to convenient belief—to what the socially and economically favored most wish or need to have believed. (TCOC, p. 95.)

When an economist argues for lower taxes on the affluent, people should be right in believing that he is speaking out of economic perception or compassion and not because he has been bought. Nor should he ever be inhibited in his speech by what a corporate client might think. These rules are now extensively honored in the breach. Numerous economists put their professional gloss on corporate propaganda, pressure for tax relief, resistance to regulation, or varied efforts to subvert the antitrust laws. And most sell out for a shockingly low sum, not being aware that a reputation can be sold only once or twice. After it becomes known that a scholar can be had for money, his market value sharply declines. (ALIOT, p. 57.)

The shortcomings of economics are not original error but uncorrected obsolescence. The obsolescence has occurred because what is convenient has become sacrosanct. Anyone who attacks such ideas must seem to be a trifle self-confident

and even aggressive. Yet I trust that judgments will not be too
hasty. The man who makes his entry by leaning against an infirm door gets an unjustified reputation for violence. Something is to be attributed to the poor state of the door.
(TAS, p. 4.)

WRITING

[Thorstein] Veblen's influence on me has lasted long. One
of my greatest pleasures in writing has come from the
thought that perhaps my work might annoy someone of com-
fortably pretentious position. Then comes the saddening
realization that such people rarely read. (ALIOT, pp. 30–31.)

I did learn that, for a young economist, publication, even on
so esoteric a subject as the preferences of consumers for or-
ange blossom honey over sage, is a prime measure of academic worth. Those passing judgment on a scholar avow
their interest in the quality of his published work, but, in the
end, most settle for counting the number of printed pages.
(ALIOT, p. 26.)

The best place to write is by yourself, because writing then
becomes an escape from the terrible boredom of your own
personality. (AOAAL, p. 288.)

To write adequately one must know, above all, how bad are
one's first drafts. They are bad because the need to combine
composition with thought, both in their own way taxing,
leads initially to a questionable, even execrable result. With
each revision the task eases, the product improves. Eventually there can be clarity and perhaps even grace. Anthony
Trollope tells proudly in his *Autobiography* that he never

sent a manuscript to his publisher without reading it over at least once with care. My commitment is to not fewer than five revisions; this, I trust, sprightly document has had six. (ALIOT, p. 535.)

In coming years I would review hundreds of volumes. After reading a book, it takes small extra effort to write down your view of it, and to do so is to impress anything that was worthy on your memory. Also, to be known as a book reviewer causes other reviewers, contemplating the reception of their own books, to be marginally more judicious. Literary survival is a multifaceted thing, and its weapons are rarely confessed. (ALIOT, p. 77.)

Originality is something that is easily exaggerated, especially by authors contemplating their own work. (TAS, p. 4.)

All authors should seek to establish a relationship of warmth, affection and mutual mistrust with their publishers in the hope that the uncertainty will add, however marginally, to compensation. (AOAAL, p. 287.)

Readers and more especially authors should be warned as to books written after sixty; the creative impulse survives more powerfully, I'm persuaded, than the critical judgment of what is written. If you continue to write, you have especially to be on guard against the tendency to plagiarize yourself. Words come to mind that are resonant in their meaning or expository power. The idea so framed is a thing of clarity and brilliance. Presently you discover, although sometimes you do not, that one reason it is so wonderful is because you have said it before. (ALIOT, p. 525.)

POLITICS

The attractions of politics are manifold, one being its theater. Politicians play roles that are larger than life and not
their own . . . A second source of interest is that politics has
come to resemble football, soccer, baseball, or any other
spectator sport. One develops, as to any contest, a commitment to the play and to the outcome. And in politics the
rankest amateur managing a campaign or working therein is
allowed to believe himself an accomplished professional . . .
For a participant, politics is also psychologically therapeutic.
Being combative, it is a solvent for aggression. One can say
things about others to an appreciative audience that normally would be reserved for private comment. This improves
personal behavior . . . Finally, with all else in politics, there is
the thought that one is helping change the world. And there
is a helpful element of illusion here. You are always aware of
your own efforts, much less so of the efforts of the many who
similarly engage themselves. From this comes a pleasantly exaggerated sense of accomplishment. It is why political memoirs must always be read with caution. (ALIOT, pp. 33–34.)

The Scotch, even when in dense mass as in Elgin County, are
the only race to which no politician ever thinks it worthwhile
to appeal. Irish, Jewish, French Canadian, Welsh, German,
Scandinavian, Ukrainian, black, and Chicano voters are so-
licited by oratory, unconvincing efforts at identification, and
inspired banality. No vote-seeker ever dons kilts, praises the
bagpipes, or utters so much as a phrase of Gaelic. It is not
entirely that such activities are considered ridiculous or
barbaric; it would appear that we have so little political
self-recognition as to make the effort not worthwhile.
(ALIOT, pp. 1–2.)

◆ ◆ ◆

Many issues of high public importance are decided by a test of bureaucratic skill. The sources of success in this arena are worth a word. One must have high confidence in one's purpose, and each step must be so taken as to enhance the confidence of others. Any mistake of the opposition must be exploited so as to weaken its credibility and support. One should remember that most Washington battles are won not out of one's own strength but from loss of confidence in others and the resulting rush to cover. One should never threaten to resign; that only tells one's allies that one might abandon the field. One should never, never accept as final the word of an expert. He can be wrong, careless, or politically motivated. Finally, one should, if possible, have the President on one's side. (ALIOT, pp. 115–116.)

Both scholarly and political life require criticism of others and invite attack or reprisal. Anyone who is initiating combat should, as a matter of elementary caution, gauge the extent and severity of the probable reaction and consider his defense. If attacked, he should promptly and strongly respond . . . [A] demonstrated capacity for reprisal serves valuably as a deterrent. (ALIOT, p. 58.)

I've told earlier of my advice to anyone so attacked. Always counterattack strongly; that may discourage your enemy and it will surely please both you and your natural allies. And by now I have formulated three supplementary rules, to wit: (1) Act promptly so as to get the same press attention as the original onslaught; (2) Do not say anything that is even marginally short of truth, for that, when exposed, undermines your whole case. Better all the damaging details; (3) Never lean to understatement. (ALIOT, p. 311.)

I will be thought too outspoken. A good diplomat, I assume, is an articulate man who articulates only what he is told. (AJ, p. 2.)

A government crisis has this in common with a sex orgy or a drunken bat: the participants greatly enjoy it although they feel they shouldn't. It exhausts them so, one having taken place, another is unlikely to follow immediately. But with the passage of time, one having occurred, there is a heightened possibility of recurrence. For men recover from their exhaustion, and memory improves on past delights. (TT, p. 124.)

POLITICIANS

Writers on [Franklin] Roosevelt speak compulsively of a father figure. My view was of a man who saw the United States as would a kindly and attentive landlord, concerned in all aspects for the lives of his tenants and the estate on which they dwelt. He was not the source of all wisdom; indeed, one considered him greatly open to petition and persuasion; and no man could ever have had more of both. But when he had decided, that was truth. (ALIOT, p. 39.)

Adlai Stevenson was committed to personality modification for public purposes . . . committed to picturing not his strength in contending with harsh circumstance but his frailty, not his certainty but his doubts, not his wisdom but the immeasurable extent of what he needed to know. So habitual had this posturing become that he was largely unaware of it himself. It was an impulse in a politician for which no one was in the slightest prepared. (ALIOT, p. 288.)

◆ ◆ ◆

Nor was great attention accorded John F. Kennedy when he arrived at Winthrop House in 1937. He too was handsome but, unlike [his brother] Joe, was gregarious, given to varied amusements, much devoted to social life and affectionately and diversely to women. One did not cultivate such students. (ALIOT, p. 53.) John F. Kennedy, as I've often told, was one of the few public men who was wholly satisfied with his own personality. It allowed him to be a constant and much amused student of the art of self-enhancement and its consequences. (ALIOT, pp. 287–288.) For those whom he trusted, Kennedy's most rewarding characteristic was his breathtaking candor — the quick chop through to truth that one immediately recognized as something to be kept in confidence. (ALIOT, p. 374.)

Nehru was standing a little apart from the throng on the spacious, very green lawn — a handsome, lean, rather small man with nicely carved features, light of complexion, as befits a Kashmiri, and wearing the white jodhpurs that were his special style. His expression was one of evident distaste for the proceedings. Later we met and talked about economics. It was a subject in which he had little interest. One was a socialist, at least in principle, and that was sufficient. (ALIOT, p. 331.)

Jacqueline Kennedy concerned herself excessively with dress and related artifacts of style. These only slightly enhanced her beauty; and they served if anything to disguise an alert and penetrating intelligence. She had always a sharper view than her husband of the people around the presidency, and while Kennedy leaned to charity, she leaned to truth. (ALIOT, p. 411.)

♦ ♦ ♦

My distance from Robert Kennedy grew out of our different capacities for political commitment. I have always tried for a measure of detachment. I've felt that one should hold some part of one's self in reserve, never be too completely sure of being right. Let belief always be tempered by discretion. None of this suited Robert Kennedy's mood; his commitment was complete. You were either for the cause or against it, either with the Kennedys or a leper. (ALIOT, p. 495.)

Johnson sought to compensate for his uncertainty in foreign policy with an outward display of firmness, strength, decisiveness. This made him open to the advice of those who urged the seemingly strong as distinct from the restrained and considered course. Perhaps also his instinct was for an assertively masculine pose, as others have suggested. Combined, these qualities put him at the mercy of those who took pride not in their knowledge but in their will to act. Thus the disaster in Southeast Asia. (ALIOT, p. 458.)

FAMILY

A few days later I married Catherine Merriam Atwater, the daughter of Alice Merriam and Charles Atwater, the latter a New York lawyer and accomplished sailor who once took his tiny craft, without radio or engine, all the way to Iceland. Kitty had been a graduate student at Radcliffe and a little earlier in Munich, an undergraduate at Smith and at the Sorbonne. She is a wise and affectionate woman of singular beauty, intensely loyal to family and friends, a superb manager of our personal affairs, a brilliant linguist and student of comparative literature, with no known enemy anywhere in the world, and we lived happily ever after. (ALIOT, p. 70.)

❖ ❖ ❖

Then came an interview with the *Hindustan Times* by a sensationally good-looking woman . . . She asked how we raised our children and why we had remained married so long. I enlarged on the need to devote as little time as possible to one's offspring lest they acquire one's bad habits; to one's virtuous tendencies, if any, they are naturally immune. I held also that marriage being a perilous and improbable association, it is safe only if the principals don't see too much of each other. She wasn't altogether persuaded but copied it down. (AOAAL, p. 255.)

PLACES

One weekend that autumn we journeyed to the Berner Oberland and went walking from the village of Gstaad, of which, until that time, neither of us had heard. This too was to have a durable effect. I was soon to find there a tranquil climate for writing which I have used ever since. It is a lovely village midway between Montreux and Interlaken in a valley where three mountain streams come together. The sun shines in; the low mountains around are shelter from the winds. Once, along with its cattle, Gstaad lived on its sawmills, and these still operate. For many years its sedentary population of around fifteen hundred has been seasonally doubled and then trebled by an influx of the fashionable rich. They have brought shops, restaurants, a swimming pool, ski-lifts, and every other amenity. They also make excellent neighbors for a writer of liberal instinct. Half are functionally illiterate and thus have no tendency to intrude on one's time. Those who can read are also deterred: "I've heard of Galbraith—some kind of Bolshevist." Often in Gstaad I have looked at the telephone and wished it would ring. (ALIOT, pp. 324–325.)

◆ ◆ ◆

Since the end of World War II, we have been coming for the summer to an old farm in southeastern Vermont. Once here, the days lengthen perceptibly. There is magic in the late evening mist on our meadows and the way the early morning sun comes through the maples. Life acquires a new tranquillity. So, we think, do the children. The pay, entertainment allowances, and other perquisites of a professor compare badly with those of industry, law, and harness racing. But it is hard to regret an occupation which enables one to spend three or four months of each year on the edge of paradise. (TLH, p.169.)

THE WISDOM OF AGE

What [finally] is happiness? The respect of good men and the affection of lovely women. (AOAAL, p. 265.)

Of late I have searched diligently to discover the advantages of age, and there is, I have concluded, only one. It is that lovely women treat your approaches with understanding rather than with disdain. And in my case that benefit came some years back. I'm now retiring a few moments ahead of statutory compulsion because I don't wish to risk similar kindness in my classes. (AVFTS, p. 129.)

The talk was of the future. I have reached the age where I comment on this with confidence, for I won't be around to hear about it if I am wrong. (AOAAL, p. 246.)

BOOK TITLES

AJ   *Ambassador's Journal* (Boston: Houghton Mifflin, 1969)

ALIOT   *A Life in Our Times* (Boston: Houghton Mifflin, 1981)

AOAAL   *Annals of an Abiding Liberal* (Boston: Houghton Mifflin, 1979)

ATP   *A Tenured Professor* (Boston: Houghton Mifflin, 1990)

AVFTS   *A View from the Stands* (Boston: Houghton Mifflin, 1986)

TAS   *The Affluent Society* (Boston: Houghton Mifflin, 1958)

TCOC   *The Culture of Contentment* (Boston: Houghton Mifflin, 1992)

TLH   *The Liberal Hour* (Boston: Houghton Mifflin, 1960)

TS   *The Scotch* (Boston: Houghton Mifflin, 1964)

TT   *The Triumph* (Boston: Houghton Mifflin, 1968)